Essentials of Macroeconomics

ESSENTIALS

OF

MACROECONOMICS

with

Moral Dilemma Commentary

Stephen M. Hotchkiss

Essentials of Macroeconomics

with Moral Dilemma Commentary

By Stephen M. Hotchkiss

ISBN: 9798693821743

Independently Published

For my loving family, all 18 of them

30 October 2020

In memory of
Prof. Ralph Chances and
to all the faculty, staff,
students and alumni who
are the Bates community

Stephen Hotchkiss '60

Essentials of Macroeconomics

TABLE OF CONTENTS

United States Economic History Backwards through Time

To give you an idea of why it is important to study and understand economic concepts and tools, let us take a walk through some economic events that occurred in the United States over the past 150 years, starting in the present and moving backward through time. This walk will touch on a few select events to underscore their importance and hopefully create a certain curiosity about their significance and why they happened. As a social science, economics is highly theoretical and consists of many concepts and tools, it also has real live value. Understanding the nature and relationships of producing and consuming goods and services will enable you to make many critically informed decisions and choices throughout your life. Keep in mind that this is a hop, skip, and jump through time and not meant to be exhaustive.

Online learning: 2020

Online learning is an educational process where both teacher and student communicate interactively via the internet. The technology has been in place for many years. Massive Open Online Courses (MOOCs) have been developed by organizations such as Coursera, TED talks, independent universities and consortia of colleges and universities. Students have had the options of taking courses in traditional face-to-face (f2f) settings or online. Courses are offered either synchronously (simultaneous interactive virtual classroom) or asynchronously (student and educator interact independently). The advent of Covid19, or coronavirus created the need for radical change. In March 2020 schools K through 12, and colleges and universities closed and sent students home. To complete their semester's course work, educators were forced to learn how to structure stimulating, creative and informative courses, utilizing lectures, manipulatives, cartoons, and graphics to motivate and educate students. Students, in turn, were required to learn a new method of education and to exercise organizational skills and discipline. What was a relatively dormant technology overnight became a common process at all levels of education.

How will this affect me?   If you are a student who relies on interaction with other students in the classroom, you may not always have this experience. If you are well-organized and disciplined you may achieve a successful education for lower cost and at your own independent pace.

Teaching point: The last chapter in this book addresses threats, opportunities, and uncertainty. The world, the marketplace, people and societies are constantly changing and evolving. Learning to manage threats, to seize opportunities, and to deal with uncertainty will lead to a much more fulfilling career.

Do you know what a bitcoin is? (2018)

Bitcoin is among the latest technology for paying or receiving monies relating to the purchase and sale of goods and services. Unlike the dollar, which is the official legal tender of the U.S. government, or any sovereign nation or government, bitcoin is a virtual form of money; that is, bitcoin is intangible and exists only in the internet cloud. Bitcoin is a digital record of financial transactions. Who uses bitcoin? People with perfectly legitimate transactions use bitcoin, and because it is unregulated, people, who are trying to hide income or wealth, buyers or sellers of goods and services who do not want the goods and services transactions recorded (money launderers, and speculators). The reward is anonymity as well as an increase in the value of a bitcoin. The risk is that the value of the bitcoin, relative to readily exchanged international currencies, may decrease dramatically and unpredictably.

How will this affect me? You may order something online and find that the seller wants to be paid in bitcoin, not dollars.

Teaching point: The chapter on Banking & Finance will explain the role of money in our economy.

What is blockchain? (2018)

Business record keeping, either of financial transactions or supply chain events, has advanced from each institution keeping its own internal records on paper or in ledger books, , to electronic management using word processing and spreadsheets, and now to an outsourced system to which multiple users have access. Outsourcing is the process of subcontracting to a third party the performance of work or functions that otherwise would be performed by employees of the firm. A block is a cluster of data about a specific transaction. It contains all of the vital details with respect to values, dates and times, goods or services, and parties engaged in the transaction. The block is then transmitted by the "chain" to all of the parties involved. Once created, the block may not be altered. This technology was made possible by the cloud. It creates opportunities for rapid transmission of data and efficient tracking of transactions.

How will this affect me? Efficiency and productivity are the primary pursuits of private enterprise in order to maximize profits. Your familiarity with technological progress will make you a more competitive professional. By the time you graduate, this technology will be standard practice.

Essentials of Macroeconomics

Teaching point: The chapters on Economic Growth and National Income will explain in depth the importance of private enterprise and increasing output of goods and services.

Have you ever seen your shadow? Could you touch your shadow? Shadow banking is real, and while it too may not be touched, it lies largely beyond the reach of governments and central banks. (2010)

There is a real, regulated and well-functioning banking system on which we all rely for safekeeping our money and granting us loans. system for support. The shadow banking system is made up of firms that attract investors' financial capital and reinvests it in a wide variety of financial instruments ranging from stocks, bonds, and derivatives such as collateralized debt obligations, commodities futures, credit default instruments or financial futures. When a firm needs to purchase a new piece of equipment, or a consumer wants to buy a house or car where would you prefer to conduct your banking, with a real bank or with a shadow bank?

How will this affect me? As your income increases, you will seek ways to save and invest your earnings. The return on your investment will reflect your willingness to undertake risk. Real banks are regulated, and insured, shadow banks are not.

Teaching point: The chapter on Investment will discuss the important roles of savings and investment in our economy.

What is a recession? (2007)

Beginning in 2007, the United States entered into a deep recession. While the recession lasted 19 months, the total output of the economy, referred to as Gross Domestic Product (GDP), declined more than 5%. Worse yet, unemployment increased to more than 10%. Even though the economy began to recover in June

2009, that recovery was slow, long and drawn out. In very simple terms, what caused the collapse was the failure of trillions of dollars invested in a variety of collateralized debt obligations in which both the real and shadow banking systems were heavily exposed.

How will this affect me? Depending on the profession you pursue, you will encounter periods of economic growth offering many opportunities, and periods of recessions when job security may be seriously threatened. Some people in our society are more vulnerable to the effects of recessions than others.

Teaching point: The chapter on Business Cycles will describe how cycles occur and what the impacts of business cycles are on the economy.

Surely you know what a ".com" enterprise is. (2001)

Silicon Valley, which by the way, exists only on paper, is the region around San Jose, Santa Clara, and south of San Francisco. It became famous because of the many start-up high technology firms that are located there. During the 1990s and up to 2000, many start-ups attracted substantial investor funds hoping to catch a windfall of returns, once the companies became profitable. There is an important point to recognize here. The investors placed their bets before the companies actually had a revenue stream for their products or services. In 2001 investor confidence broke, and with it the market for shares in those ".com" companies collapsed. As a result, many of the companies themselves failed. Some examples are: Boo.com, an online clothing retailer. Broadband Sports, a network of sports content websites. eToys .com, an online toy retailer.

How will this affect me? Are you an entrepreneur? Do you want to start your own business? What will you produce and who will buy it? Where will you find investors for your enterprise? Will people invest before your business is profitable?

Essentials of Macroeconomics

Teaching point: The chapter on Supply and Demand will explore how US producers and consumers interact to achieve mutual goals of satisfaction and rewards.

What on earth is a government surplus? (1998)

When a firm generates more funds than it spends it produces a profit. When a government receives more revenue, for example, from taxes, tariffs, and fees, than it spends, let's say on social services, defense, and government services, the result is called a surplus. Between 1998 and 2000, the US government actually produced a revenue surplus. Instead of borrowing to make up for the difference between revenue and expenses, the government was in a position to reduce its debt. What is the national debt? It is the accumulation of annual budget deficits. As of June 2020, it was about $21 trillion or 105% of GDP and rising.

How will this affect me? The old expression about the two certainties in life: Death and taxes apply to us all. The taxes you pay will, in all likelihood, be less than what the government spends. To fill in the gap, the government will borrow more money, and your taxes will likely increase. What services do you think are essential, accessible, and affordable for all Amercians?

Teaching point: The chapter on Government will explain the role of government and how it works.

Who ever heard of inflation? (1980)

Has the dollar you earned last year and put into a savings account enabled you to buy the same smart phone for the same price? That's a tough question because each new generation of smart phones has different features so that the price changes. But, if you replaced a smart phone with an exact duplicate, the price probably did not change much. If it had, that would be because the cost of making the phone had increased or the value of your dollar had decreased. Between 1974 and 1983, a period of ten years, the purchasing power of the dollar was cut in half. That is to say, it took twice as many dollars to buy something in 1983 as that same item cost in 1974.

How will this affect me? Unless your income increases at a rate greater the rise in the cost of living, each year your purchasing power will decrease. You will be able to afford less and less. Are some people more negatively impacted by inflation than others?

Teaching point: The discussion of the role of money in our economy will provide a deeper understanding about how currencies increase, retain, or lose value.

If you move from Ohio to Florida, can you still find an office of Chase, Bank of America, or Wells Fargo around the corner? (1970)

Well, maybe you can, or maybe you can't. Prior to 1970 it could not happen. Banks were only allowed to have branches in their home state. From a consumer perspective, it is convenient to keep banking with the same bank. From the bankers' point of view, it means growth and diversity opportunities. Beginning in the 1980s, states deregulated banks and opened the doors to interstate banking. It has led to a huge concentration of assets and deposits controlled by the ten largest banks in the country. They control more than 60% of assets, and 50% of deposits. Conversely, about 5,000 banks hold the remaining 40% of assets and 50% of deposits.

How will this affect me? If you move you may choose to stay with the same bank, but be removed from the decision-makers, and subject to nationwide standard policies and pricing.

Essentials of Macroeconomics

Teaching point: Chapters on Banking and Finance will enable you to make more informed decisions and choices as you change locations.

How important is economic growth?

World War II lasted for six years, 1939 to 1945. It was fought in two theaters: Europe and Asia. 56.4 million people lost their lives. If you are interested, 26.6 million were Russians and 0.4 million were Americans. The devastation was so great that the only significant industrial economy to survive was that of the United States. Continental Europe, the UK, and Japan were destroyed. The immediate period after the war witnessed an economic contraction in the US while our industrial capacity was converted from war production to that of domestic goods. During the war no cars were manufactured for consumers. Gasoline was rationed and food supplies were adequate but limited. Beginning in 1947, the US embarked on one of the greatest economic growth periods in our history. Jobs were plentiful. Family incomes increased. Production of housing and consumer goods expanded dramatically.

How will this affect me? With an increasing population, economic growth is essential to produce more jobs and professional opportunities.

Teaching points: The chapter on Measuring the Economy discusses at length the importance of economic growth and how it is achieved.

What is the difference between the great recession of 2007 and the depression of the 1930s?

Technically, a recession occurs when economic output decreases two consecutive quarters. A depression, therefore, is a very deep, prolonged recession. The recession of 2007 endured 19 months. The great depression of the 1930s endured over ten years. Industrial output decreased 30%. Agricultural output declined initially by 60%, and unemployment reached 25%. In spite of multiple government efforts, it was WWII that brought the US out of the depression.

How will this affect me? Events, such as a depression are beyond individual control, but, when and if they happen, the importance of conservative living, saving money, and minimizing debt becomes very critical.

Teaching point: The chapter discussing business cycles explores in depth causes of past recessions and depressions, and ways in which the government and central bank might ameliorate them.

Do we take life-changing inventions for granted?

Between the late 19th century and 1940 at least nine significant life changing inventions were not only created but mass produced. The elevator permitted high rise buildings. The telephone enabled immediate transfer of information. Electricity replaced oil lamps and the development of electrically powered devices. The stove replaced wood-burning fireplaces. Radios enabled mass communication of news and entertainment for all, those literate and those not. Refrigerators permitted the storage of food. The automobile replaced the horse and buggy. Movies provided entertainment for masses of people. The clothes washer freed people, primarily women, from time-consuming household chores. For people living in that era, life became significantly more comfortable and new horizons were opened.

How will this affect me? We have lived with these inventions for so long that we may take them for granted. They may seem like ancient history. Those inventions occurred over a 60-year period. Today, invention and innovation seem to occur in milliseconds, but how life-changing are they? How adaptable will you have to be personally and professionally? How vulnerable is my job or profession to unexpected technological change, and how can I prepare for it?

Essentials of Macroeconomics

Teaching point: Several chapters about Markets, Income Distribution, and the Mixed Economy will shed light on this topic.

How did the industrial revolution change the size and shape of the US economy?

Imagine living on a farm. If you lived in the 1800, the odds were almost 9:10 that you lived on a farm. You got up with the sunrise and went to bed with the sunset. You sweated in the summer and froze in the winter. You were lucky to get a 6th grade education, married the girl next door, and lived and died within a hundred miles of where you were born. The major accomplishment of the industrial revolution was mastering steam power, which led to the invention of steam engines for railroads, mass production of goods, labor specialization, standard component sizes, and the location of factories near essential resources such as coal, iron ore, and people. By the turn of the 20th century the odds of living and working on a farm were reduced to .02:10.

How will this affect me? The likelihood of your profession changing radically or of you changing professions over a 40-year career is increasing exponentially. The likelihood of dedicating an entire career to one employer is significantly less than it was 20 years ago. To maintain your competitiveness, life-time professional development will be critical to your success.

Teaching point: Understanding economic concepts and tools will enable you to analyze and reach informed critical conclusions throughout your life.

The above thirteen events by no means cover all of the economic events of the last two centuries. Their significance is in their making. Each one puts a different economic concept or tool to the test.

One last thought, back to the present:

Essentials of Macroeconomics

What is "creative destruction"? The term is almost self-defining. It is a concept created by a famous economist, Joseph Schumpeter. Answer the following question: What is it that does not take lunch breaks, does not call in sick, or take vacations, and is able to perform repeated functions tirelessly and consistently?

We are living in the age of robot technology. Robots are complex machines programed to perform a wide range of functions, often independently, but also with human input and instruction. Robots replace people, they destroy the traditional way in which products and services are produced. At the same time, they produce new opportunities, are less costly, and generate higher quality outputs. All sorts of products we consume are produced by robots. Applications include: manufacturing (autos), assembly and packing, laboratory research, weaponry and surgery, as a few examples. How many "robo-calls" do you receive on your smart phone? Combined with artificial intelligence, we are on the cusp of an entirely new wave of technology.

How will this affect me? With the rapid development of new technologies, in determining your career, you must take into consideration the potential impact of changes in technology on your chosen profession. A good rule of thumb is asking the question, "Can this function be digitized'?

Teaching point: The chapter on Resource Utilization will describe in detail the changing relationships between land, labor and capital.

Introduction

What is economics?

The traditional definition of Economics is a social science dedicated to study and analysis of how to satisfy insatiable wants with scarce resources.

What are insatiable wants?

The answer depends on who you are, where you live, and what your needs and expectations might be. For example, India, a country about one-third the size of the continental United States, has a population four times that of the U.S. or 1.2 billion people. Of those 1.2 billion, 250 million or 20% urinate and defecate at large (e.g., they have no sanitary facilities).

Contrast that with the most expensive penthouse cooperative apartment in New York City, which recently sold for $238 million. The unit has 24,000 square feet, with more bedrooms, bathrooms and entertaining area than can be imagined.

Do you drive a Ford Focus or a Lamborghini? Do you vacation in the Caribbean or drive to a relative's home? Do you dine out frequently, or do you eat at home, or are you even able to put a full meal on the table?

Is there a difference between wants and needs?

Usually, we define needs as those items such as food, clothing, and shelter. In this 21st century, many would add access to affordable healthcare and education, heat and air conditioning, television, computers, and cell phones. Make your own list.

On the other hand, while needs are necessities, wants are luxuries. Wants are items we might be able to live without. Wants are Champagne and caviar as opposed to meat and potatoes; fancy brand clothing instead of basic jeans and shirts; a ten-room house instead of three bedrooms and a living/dining and kitchen area; and yes, a Lamborghini instead of a Ford Focus.

What are scarce resources?

Traditionally, economics defines resources as land, labor, and capital. Land encompasses air, water, and land contents such as rich soil, minerals, trees, flowers, and all things related thereto. Labor is both human beings and human capital. Human beings are those among us who inhabit the earth, regardless of our gender, age, or physical or mental abilities. Human capital refers to level of education, skills and acquired ability to perform work.

All of the above, in one form or another, are scarce. Air is abundant, but breathable, pure air is scarce and expensive. Air, free of pollution can only be found in rural, out-of-the-way places. Air in urban areas must be treated to cleanse the pollution.

The world population is 7.3 billion people. Approximately 1.4 billion live in the Peoples' Republic of China (PRC). Another 1.2 billion live in India. By contrast, 420 million live in the 29 countries making up the European Union, and 328 million live in the United States. But for the fact that people are scattered all over the earth with large portions concentrated in urban areas, one might say that human beings are not scarce. However, when considering the human capital factor, one encounters a great disparity of levels of education and acquired skills to meet the productive needs of nations and the world.

Finally, capital, which from an economic point of view is defined as plant and equipment, to which I add technology, is also very scarce. Plant and equipment are factors of production and are man's creation of combining labor and land. It is capital, which enabled the United States to transfer 90% of its population from the farm to urban dwellings and commerce and industry. It is the lack of capital, plant and equipment which contributes to the poverty of those 250 million in India, of people living at subsistence levels in Africa, Latin America and Southeast Asia. Conversely, it is the increased access to capital that has enabled the PRC to emerge from massive poverty to a country with many people living above the poverty level and beginning to enjoy the fruits of their labors.

What is the difference between macroeconomics and microeconomics?

As the prefix "macro" implies, it is the study of the sum of the whole economy; The totality or aggregate perspective of a universe or system. One might view macro as looking from the top down, as opposed to from the bottom up. Macroeconomics is the study of the basic principles, tools, hypotheses, rules or laws that pertain to the entire sphere of economic behavior.

In the same manner "micro" is the study of individual components that affect or contribute to economic behavior. While in macroeconomics we analyze and evaluate the larger picture from measuring performance of the whole economy, what drives human consumption, what motivates production, the role of finance and global economic impacts; in microeconomics we analyze and evaluate consumer and producer behavior and their responses to changes in price and elasticity, cost and revenue factors, the structure of markets, factors influencing labor supply and demand, and the roles of rent, profits, and interest.

Why is economics referred to as a social science?

Social sciences are those sciences which focus on the study of human behavior, its origins, factors influencing it, and both historical and likely future consequences. Physical sciences are more concrete and measure inputs such as weights and measures, volume, molecular composition, muscular and structural components. Chemistry, physics, biology, and anatomy are some examples of physical sciences.

Especially with the development of information technology, many economic factors and patterns of behavior have been and are being quantified. Within economics, the field of econometrics has literally exploded. Nevertheless, the human factor, the challenge of understanding the influence of nature versus nurture in human behavior still befuddle economic analysis and predictability.

As a social science, what are the ethical and moral values embedded in economics?

The answer is that there are none. Economics is an amoral science; that is, economics is a study with concepts, hypotheses, tools, laws and rules which are devoid of moral or ethical considerations. That doesn't suggest that economists themselves are amoral or not ethical people, but rather that the social science itself does not entertain ethical or moral standards or mores.

At the conclusion of each chapter is a section entitled "Moral Dilemmas." The purpose of these sections is precisely to ask questions and raise issues relating to the consequences of economic decision making.

Moral Commentary

If we accept the premise that as a social science, macroeconomics is amoral, it means that economics is neutral with respect to moral or ethical issues, standards or values. That being the case, we must ask the question: How do moral issues and values apply?

The application of economic concepts, hypotheses, and principles requires the collection of data, its validation, analysis, conclusions, recommendations, decisions, and execution of those decisions. All of the above requires human intervention. A unique attribute to us as humans is the ability to reason. Inherent in that ability is the responsibility to behave in a moral manner and to be held accountable for our acts as rational, moral human beings.

Furthermore, another question should be asked and answered. Is it the purpose of the economy to serve the people (society), or is it the role of people or society to serve the economy? This distinction is important because for a valid discussion of moral standards and value to occur, we need to agree that it is the role of the economy to serve people and society.

Moral standards and values according to whom?

The subject of Essentials of Macroeconomics with a Moral Commentary is the United States economic system. That system has evolved from western civilization and a population which largely reflects a Judeo-Christian heritage. In the Old Testament, commandments five through ten deal with mans' relationship with fellow mankind: Honor thy parents, Do not kill, Do not commit adultery, Do not bear false witness, and Do not covet. In the New Testament, those six commandments are synthesized in one: Love thy neighbor as thyself. The saying, "Do unto others as you would have them do unto you," is an expression of the same principle.

In a more universal context, one can examine the great religions and encounter the same moral values.

- Islam: Commit virtuous deeds. Avoid evil and vice. Do not be vain. Do not accumulate wealth.

- Hindu: Do not harm others in word or deed. Do not steal or covet. Be celibate when single. Refrain from lying.

- Native American: Treat all men with respect. Demean no one. Touch nothing not yours.

- Buddhism: Take responsibility for your own fortunes and misfortunes. Avoid evil. Do good.

- Shintoism: Be benevolent. Promote the public good. Respect the law. Trust and be trusted by friends.

In each of the following chapters there will be a discussion of the moral implications of the chapter topic. The purpose of the discussion will be to raise questions and an awareness that no data collection, validation, analysis, conclusions, recommendations and decisions can be done without examining the costs and benefits of the decisions and both direct and indirect consequences on society as a whole and its individual parts.

To facilitate this discussion, I shall borrow the term *stakeholder*. This term was originally applied to expand the objective of the firm from maximizing shareholder value to include a host of other parties with whom the firm engages or upon whom a firm's activity may have an impact.

In the broader context, stakeholders are all 328 million of us. From an economic impact point of view, there are many subsets of stakeholders, for example:

- Gender: Male, Female, Intersex
- Sexual Orientation: Cisgender, LGBTQ
- Age: Young, Middle Age, Elder
- Geographic: Urban, Rural, East, Midwest, West, North, South
- Marital status: Married, Single, Partner
- Race/Ethnicity: White, Black, of color, Asian, Latino, Native American
- Nationality: US, North American, Latin American, Western European, African, Asian, Sub-Continent, Southeast Asia, Oceania
- Education: High School, College, Graduate School
- Skills: Unskilled, Semi-skilled, Skilled, Professional
- Abilities: Abled, Disabled

- Employment status: Full time, Part time, Gig or Occasional, Unemployed
- Sector: Agriculture, Industry, Hospitality, Health care, Finance, Education, Government

Why identify so many subsets?

The collection of data, its analysis, validation, conclusions, and recommendations all reflect the complexity of our society and have diverse impacts on each segment or sub-set. It is critical that these issues be addressed fully in order to determine what the likely direct and indirect consequences of an economic decision are most likely to be. Each of the following chapters will conclude with a moral commentary raising these issues for critical consideration by you, the reader.

Chapter 1: Gross Domestic Product

Gross domestic product is just a number. At the time of this writing, it happens to be $21.7 trillion. That is $21,700,000,000,000. This number can be at the beginning of an analysis or at the conclusion. It is not an exact number, but rather a statistical estimate. It can be statistically accurate, such as is the case in the U.S. or Western Europe, or it can be a less reliable estimate such as is the case of the Peoples' Republic of China or India. GDP can be relative to reflect the fact that the U.S. GDP is 22% of global GDP, and it can be relevant as a measure of economic health of a country.

What is Gross Domestic Product and how is it measured?

Gross Domestic Product (GDP) is the expenditure of total final goods and services produced by an economy in the course of one year. It is the sum of Consumption (what do we spend on goods and services), Investment (what do we save and then invest in plant and equipment), Government (What do the federal, state and local governments spend), and Net Exports (what is the difference between total exports, a plus, and total imports, a minus). GDP = C + I + G + Xn. In 2018, those components were $20 trillion (100%) = $14.4 (72%) + $2.2 (11%) + $4.2 (21%) + -$0.8 (-4%). The negative Xn indicates that we exported less than we imported.

Essentials of Macroeconomics

If one subtracts depreciation, which is the measure of wear and tear or lost value of plant and equipment, one derives net domestic product. Likewise, if one subtracts depreciation from gross investment, one derives net investment.

What is the importance of Gross Domestic Product?

Imagine trying to manage a business without knowing what its total productive capacity was? Not only would you not be able to determine total output, but you would not be able to increase, decrease or balance inputs to reach that optimum output.

The GDP is only a number, but it is a very significant number for a variety of reasons. Prior to the pandemic crisis of 2020 in the United States, there were 6.3 million people unemployed. There were estimated to be another 6 million people under- employed (people with jobs that either do not fully utilize their skills or are occasional or part-time). As a result of the pandemic, unemployment rose to 22 million people. Plant and equipment were at about 80% of *capacity utilization*. With a population of 328 million, the GDP per capita was $67 thousand. What this information indicates is that GDP should be at a level of $21 trillion to perform at its optimum level. That is to say that to provide employment opportunities for all 160 million workers, the GDP needs to increase by more fully using other resources, namely plant, equipment and land, the two economic resources complementing labor.

Capacity utilization is an estimate of the percentage of potential total output of a production facility is actually being used. For example, if an auto assembly plant is at 80%, output may be increased another 20%, before additional plant and equipment must be constructed and installed.

Essentials of Macroeconomics

What is included in the calculation of GDP?

As a statistical estimate, GDP attempts to measure the total output of all final goods and services in a particular year. It is a dynamic number. As obsolete products cease to be produced, they disappear from the GDP calculation. As new products are invented or innovated, they are included. During recessions it is common that fewer new products are manufactured and that consumers service and repair old products to save money. This change in economic behavior is reflected in GDP. Consequently, as stated at the introduction of this chapter, GDP must be viewed as one number among many to measure more effectively the real output of an economy.

To attempt to improve on the measure and quality of economic output, economists developed the concept of an Economic Progress Indicator (EPI). This measure includes housework and volunteer work while continuing to exclude illegal and underground activity. The revised concept takes into consideration externalities such as environmental issues, resource depletion and family breakdown. The EPI serves as another statistic or number in the overall evaluation of economic performance.

What are some factors to avoid in compiling GDP?

A critical word in the definition of GDP is "final." It is assumed that all costs contributing to the production of a final good or service are included in its ultimate price or total cost. One could accumulate the costs of all component parts as value added to the final product. That process would be cumbersome and complicated. A good or product is counted only at the first point of sale. Thereafter, it is considered a used, or "previously owned" product and not added to GDP.

Financial transactions and transfer payments are also excluded from GDP. These functions do not add productive value. Financial transactions facilitate the transfer of title, ownership, or use. Transfer payments occur without the requirement of rendering work or adding value.

What is the importance of measuring GDP in terms of real value or expenditures?

The words "nominal" and "real" are used to distinguish between prices at current levels and prices indexed to reflect a change in the purchasing power of a currency (dollar). The reduction in purchasing power is caused by inflation and is measured by the Consumer Price Index. Inflation is a measure of an increase in the general level of prices. It reflects lost purchasing power and is sometimes referred to as "too many dollars chasing too few goods." It is important to measure GDP in terms of constant or real dollars, otherwise, GDP will be artificially inflated by the additional dollars required to purchase a product due to the lost purchasing power of the currency.

As an example, say last year you bought a suit or a dress for $100. With a rate of inflation of 2.5%, the same suit or dress will cost $102.50 this year. If it costs less, then some increase in productivity or other reduced cost of a raw material enabled the manufacturer to produce the suit or dress for less. Likewise, if the cost is greater than $102.50, some factor of production also increased the cost. From your point of view, the product (the suit or dress), is the same. In measuring GDP, the nominal or current price is adjusted by the inflation factor to determine the real value in constant dollars.

The Consumer Price Index (CPI) is calculated using a base year, 1983, as 100. The CPI in 2020 was 258. In 1983 nominal and real GDP were $3.4 trillion. In 2020, nominal GDP was $21.7 trillion. When calculating real GDP, in other words, adjusting for inflation, the number becomes $8.4 trillion (21.7/258=8.4). However, the United States Department of Labor introduced the concept of chained dollars in 2005. Chained dollars are a logarithmic expansion of CPI. The base year is

2005 instead of 1983. The adjusted value between nominal GDP at 100: $12.4 trillion in 2005 and nominal GDP of $20 trillion in 2020 yields a real GDP of $17.5 trillion.

How does the United States GDP compare with other countries?

In 2019 global GDP was about $142 trillion, the United States portion of that number being 21.4. At that time, the number exceeded the total GDP of Japan, and China (14.0 and 5.1 respectively, with Germany at 3.9 for a total of 23.0.

What is the meaning of per capita real GDP?

Of course, we all know that the per capita GDP is derived by dividing total real GDP by the population. In this case, we divide $21.4 trillion/328 million to confirm that the per capita GDP $65,847. Does that mean that each man, woman and child earns $67,812? No! Like many statistical measurements, it does indicate whether or not the Gross Domestic Product is growing at a rate less than or greater than the rate of growth of the population. 2019 GDP per capita is significantly greater than numbers of previous decades. The purchasing power of the dollar and income distribution will be discussed in later chapters. The importance of measuring income per capita serves as a starting point to determine income distribution. For example, as indicated in chapter sixteen, the lowest income quintile averages $24,600, and the highest quintile $237,000.

What is GDP missing as a measure of economic well-being?

Because it is difficult to quantify the value added of certain functions in our economy, they are not included in the calculation of GDP. Such functions include:

1.   Illegal production and the underground economy: In any economy there are certain activities that occur outside the formal economy. These activities include production and sales of street drugs, contraband, prostitution, and off-the-books services to avoid taxes.

2.   Volunteer work: One of the finest aspects of the U.S. economy and society is the amount of volunteer work carried on by many religious and secular organizations. The lives of those less fortunate are significantly enhanced by such endeavors, and yet those efforts are not included.

3.   Leisure time: The forty-hour work week was introduced in the 1930s. The five-day work week is a post WWII achievement. Living ten to 15 years beyond one's retirement is also a phenomenon of the past 25 years. There is no quantitative accounting for such qualitative gains in health and well-being.

4.   Product changes and human costs and benefits: GDP does not take into consideration changes or modifications in product features or qualities. A modern car has many more features and lasts considerably longer than did a car manufactured in the 1960s. The cost and quality of grocery store food has improved nutritionally and decreased in cost. On the other hand, the stress of commuting, competing to maintain one's employment, and the disparity between high paying jobs and low paying jobs has increased significantly over the past thirty years. None of these factors is included in the calculation of GDP or GDP per capita.

Summary

Gross Domestic Product (GDP) is the initial step or overall means of measuring economic activity. By calculating the cost of producing final goods and services, the need to evaluate intermediate goods and services is eliminated, as their costs are incorporated in the final output. GDP has a number of shortcomings such as failure to take into consideration changes in quality, technology or features in a final output. Duration or product life is also not considered. Certain economic activities, such as household work. volunteer work, and illegal activities are also ignored. GDP and per capita GDP do serve as an important starting point for analyzing economic behavior and evaluating different sectors and contributors to overall economic performance.

Moral Dilemmas:

1.   Does reliance on GDP statistical data cause distortion in interpretation of data and economic policy discussions?

2.   Are those factors excluded from GDP calculations, homemakers, volunteers, black market traders demeaned or diminished by this exclusion?

3.   Should GDP attempt to include issues such as quality of life, environmental impact, and disparate income distribution?

4.   Will GDP policy discussions have equal or unequal impacts on various sectors of the economy, various geographic centers, and various demographic sectors of the country?

Moral Commentary

The following comments are not meant to be exhaustive, but rather to address certain issues that are critical to understand what purposes GDP data serves and what it fails to serve.

1.   GDP data measures outputs, not inputs. While, in a competitive economy it is assumed that producers will seek the most efficient and cost-effective combination of inputs (resources), whether or not these uses reflect the highest and best uses of those resources is not measured. Likewise, resource depletion is not addressed. For example, as a result of the electrification of America in the 1920s and 30s, the supply of copper was entirely depleted resulting in our reliance on imports from Chile and Bolivia. Is it in the national interest to measure and

manage these issues? Are precious resources used to produce frivolous goods? If so, who decides what is frivolous?

2.   With industrialization and continuous introduction of new technology, capital has increasingly replaced labor. Until the past 20 years, the United States experienced a significant increase in productivity. The savings realized in producing more goods at lower costs does not address the indirect costs borne by society in the manner of retraining workers or providing unemployment compensation and health coverage. If producers generate these costs, should they bear some of the related indirect costs?

3.   Spillovers or externalities are costs and/or benefits incurred by third parties as a result of actions taken by first parties or producers. For example, if a farmer uses chemicals such as fertilizers or insecticides that penetrate the ground and with rainwater runoff into streams, rivers and lakes, the cost of the pollution is borne by those downstream. The water is contaminated, unsuitable for drinking, endangers marine life, and inhibits recreational use. Should not GDP measure these negative burdens?

Chapter 2: Economics According to Keynes

The concept of a nation-state emerged in the 17th century, when mercantilism, the emphasis on exports exceeding imports to accumulate wealth, prevailed in economic thinking. The 18th century was a tumultuous period for Britain, France, and the United States. While Ben Franklin published "Poor Richard's Almanac," the French produced the first *Encyclopedia*. James Watt invented the steam engine and Eli Whitney invented the cotton gin. At the same time, wars were waged throughout Europe: The War of the Spanish Succession; the Seven Years War, or as known in the United States, the French and Indian War; the American Revolution and the French Revolution. France lost Spain and its North American Colonies and Britain lost its North American colonies. Britain added India to its empire and, at the end of the era, Napoleon emerged to build a new France.

What do all of these events tell us about the 18th century? It was a period culminating in the rise of cities resulting from increased migration from rural areas. It was also a period of greater production of goods in an urban setting, of a decrease in the role of the self-sustaining farm, and of greater interdependence among workers in the preindustrial era. While the invention of the steam engine ignited the industrial revolution, that embarkation was just beginning. More importantly, with greater concentration of population in cities, the have-nots realized what a vast gulf had been created between themselves and the very rich. The proletariat overthrew the bourgeois. Philosophers and economists were examining factors of production and analyzing the roles of workers, consumers, and entrepreneurs.

Adam Smith, the father of economics and a humanist, argued that specialization, the division of labor, and people acting out of rational self-interest in a competitive economy would produce economic prosperity. Enter Jean Baptiste Say, a French economist and entrepreneur. Say was a committed *laissez-faire* economist, who developed a theory known as Say's Law, which simply states that "Supply creates its own demand." Now, if you are talking about something obscure, perhaps the law does not make a lot of sense. On a more practical level, however, if one speaks of cattle for beef, shoes for horses or bricks for houses, the production of these goods satisfies a human want which in turn, makes the product marketable. In return for selling the product, the producer receives a payment which is then applied to purchase another product and thus the process is repeated to fulfill the concept, "Supply creates its own demand."

Laissez faire is a French term which literally translates to 'let do'. Economists use the term to describe a "hands off" or non-government interventionist policy with respect to economic performance.

What is the role of consumption?
In this context, one could argue that GDP = Consumption. That is, if everyone spent everything they earned, then GDP would be equal to consumption. What happens if an individual or society does not spend its entire earnings on consumption, but rather sets aside some earnings for savings?

What is the role of savings?
Let us assume that money is not stored in a mattress; rather, as savings, money is deposited in a bank in return for which one receives earnings called interest. Bankers can pay interest only if they are able to lend the money to individuals and

firms that in turn will invest the funds in plant, equipment, and inventory. That is to say, the money must be put to some use for it to be productive.

What is the relationship between savings and investments?

Now the formula for GDP becomes more complex, for GDP = C + S, where S = I (savings equal investments). Is that a realistic assumption to make? Yes, because both savings and investments behave the same as any ordinary goods or services. Savings are the supply side of the equation where investments are the demand side. If the demand for savings increases then the cost of funds, interest rates, rises. The increase in the interest rates attracts more savings, which in turn, causes interest rates to decline, because supply now exceeds demand. In this trial and error exercise, eventually an equilibrium rate between savings and investments results.

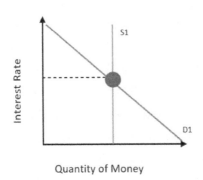

Quantity of Money

In the event of two extremes, inadequate savings to satisfy the demand for investments or too much savings far exceeding the demand for investments, interest rates would either reach levels that would deter further investment, or fall to such low levels as to deter savings. That is to say, market forces, over time, will cause the two factors to return to an equilibrium point.

What is a classical equilibrium?

As demonstrated in the above graph, at a macroeconomic level, when (aggregate) quantity demanded equals the (aggregate) quantity supplied there is equilibrium. This balance of opposing forces should, therefore, show no tendency to change. Underlying this concept is the assumption that the economy is approaching full employment, and that government has no role to play.

What is the implication with respect to aggregate demand and aggregate supply?

A simple demand curve demonstrates an inverse relationship between price and quantity demanded. As price falls the quantity demanded increases, and vice versa. Aggregate demand is that demand representing the total value of real GDP that all sectors of the economy are willing to purchase at various price levels. In a sense, aggregate demand is the sum of all individual demand curves. Keep in mind that consumers are likely to buy more of something when the price is low and less when it is high.

A simple supply curve demonstrates a direct relationship between price and the quantity produced. As price rises the quantity supplied increases, and vice versa. Aggregate supply is that supply representing the total value of real output that will be made available by producers or sellers at various price levels. As opposed to consumers, it is suppliers who respond directly to a change in price. Suppliers or producers of goods and services will produce more at a higher price and less at a lower price. This is why the price/supply relationship is direct.

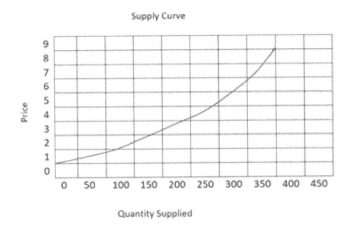

What is the real balance effect?

In the aggregate, a general rise in prices essentially causes a decrease in purchasing power. Instead of diverting consumption from one good to another, total demand or total consumption must decrease. Conversely, a general decrease in prices causes an increase in purchasing power. Total demand, or total consumption, will increase (*all things being equal* if money is not diverted to savings).

All things being equal is a term frequently used in the study of economics. It is a concept of isolating a variable factor and leaving everything else in suspension, or unchanged. While in the actual economy that concept may not be realistic, it serves a point in describing likely behavior or responses to economic phenomena.

What is the interest rate effect?

However, all things are not equal, and an increase in consumption will cause prices to rise as supply lags demand. This imbalance between demand and supply will lead to a demand for investment funds to expand productive capacity and thereby satisfy the increasing consumption. Such demand for investment funds will cause interest rates to rise and thereby induce consumers to spend less of their disposable income and save more. Should the decline in consumption be significant or endure for an extended period of time, the combination of reduced consumption and rising interest rates will disrupt the investment process.

What is the foreign purchases effect?

Put very simply, if prices of goods and services increase beyond a certain point, United States' consumers will seek goods and services from foreign sources. This tendency will lead to a change in the purchasing power of different currencies, which, in turn, will mitigate the trend. This phenomenon will be amplified in later chapters.

Why is the long-run aggregate supply curve vertical?

A vertical supply curve means that there can be no increase in output regardless of a change in price. A vertical supply curve also means that all factors of production have been exhausted. That is, no additional land, labor, or capital will increase output. Bear in mind that classical economists were working on the assumption of reaching full employment.

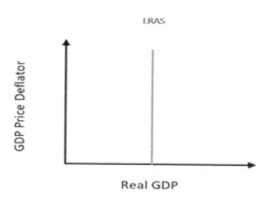

Essentials of Macroeconomics

Why does the short-run aggregate supply curve gradually incline?

In the very short-run, producers are able to increase output without incurring increased marginal costs of production. Marginal costs are those costs relating to the production of one or more additional units of output. In the event that demand continues to increase then the effort to satisfy the increase, in the short-run, requires the employment of more expensive land, labor, and capital; thus, the curve inclines to reflect the higher prices incurred and passed on to consumers. Eventually, the short-run aggregate supply curve will become vertical as reflected in the long-run supply curve.

What does Keynes think about the classical economists' views?

The revolutions of the 19th century were fought over the outrageous disparities between the rich, who had plenty, and the poor, who had nothing. Wars, on the other hand, are fought over real estate. WWI, for example, was fought over maintaining possession of or gaining access to coal, iron, oil and gas. John Maynard Keynes (1885 – 1946) lived during the events of the Russian Revolution, WWI, the expansion and excesses of post WWI economies in parts of Western Europe and the United States, and the Great Depression of the 1930s. Keynes rejected a number of the assumptions argued by classical economists. He disagreed with the notions of *laissez-faire*, that supply creates its own demand, that full employment was a sustainable condition, that savings and investments always tended to be equal, and that there was no economic role for government.

On the concept of *laissez-faire*, Keynes argued that market forces would not always correct economic deficiencies. If supply creates its own demand, why are there depressions? Economies go through periods of under-employment, full employment, and over-employment. At times savings exceed investments and at times savings are insufficient to meet investment demand. He concluded that government, which is not driven by the profit motive, plays a unique role in trying to maintain economic stability.

Essentials of Macroeconomics

What are the components of the Keynesian System?

Keynes' primary argument is that demand or consumption is the primary driving force in an economy, but not the exclusive force. In fact, he argued that demand creates supply, not the other way around. The Keynes short-term supply curve begins at a horizontal level, increases over time as demand continues to increase, and, eventually, becomes vertical, when all but one factor of production can be changed. It was Keynes who articulated the distinction between Consumption, Investments, Government, and Net Exports as the components of Gross Domestic Product.

What are the relationships among consumption, savings, and investments?

Individuals have two choices with respect to disposable income: One is to spend or consume, and the other is to save. Individuals with low incomes in fact have no choice. All of their income is spent on consumption. Those individuals with higher income levels do, indeed, have choices to make. When prices increase, individuals with low income suffer a loss of purchasing power. People of higher income can adjust their spending patterns and may also choose to save less.

In addition, during periods of economic recession, when firms allow production facilities to remain underutilized, the investment demand decreases causing interest rates to decline as well. The decline in interest rates leads to a decline in savings. During periods of economic expansion production facilities run at full capacity and firms increase their demand for investments, causing interest rates to increase. This causes an increase in savings. These changes in the business cycle are demonstrated in examples of underutilization of resources, and periods of stress, when resources are stretched beyond their normal capacity.

How does an economy flow from disequilibrium to equilibrium?

If aggregate demand exceeds aggregate supply, two consequences will result: First, there will be a tendency toward price inflation, as there are not enough goods and services to satisfy consumer demand. Second, firms will enjoy excess profits. In either case, existing firms and new entrants to the marketplace will increase production, eventually bringing supply in line with demand, at which point there is equilibrium.

It is more than likely that, once the equilibrium point is reached, firms will continue to expand production. The result will be a condition in which aggregate supply exceeds aggregate demand. The consequence of this condition will be to reverse the process described above. Firms will slow down production, and resources, which may have been utilized beyond their normal capacity, will become under-utilized. The economy will falter and enter a recessionary period.

What is the role of Government?

Government provides a number of services which the private sector is either unable or unwilling to produce. There are obvious functions of government such as national defense, regulation of commerce, and maintaining public order through public safety and a judicial system, which pertain to the public or government sector. There are a number of other services which might just as easily be performed by the public sector or the private sector, such as education, libraries, parks, and infrastructure. In any event, to provide these services, the government generates revenue through taxes and then spends the proceeds.

It is Keynes' argument that, during periods of economic expansion, the government should reduce its expenditures and increase taxes, thus, in fact, generating a budgetary surplus. Furthermore, during periods of economic contraction or recession, the government should increase its expenditures and reduce taxes. In this manner, during periods of economic growth the public sector retreats and allows the private sector to be the engine of growth. During periods of recession, when the private sector has no incentive to continue production, the government should step in and fill the gap, creating employment opportunities and increasing disposable income, and thereby consumer demand, via employment income and reduced taxes.

Summary

The thoughts, theories and influence of economists are a direct reflection of the times in which they live, the stage of development of the economies and societies, and their access to economic information. During the 19th century, the primary focus of economic thinking was on the relationships of workers to changing economic forces, urbanization, specialization, increased production and to the owners of industry. During the first part of the 20th century the focus of economic thinking changed to focus more on macroeconomic forces such as why did consumption and savings fluctuate over periods of time and during the ebb and flow of business cycles. What influence did investment have on aggregate savings? Did the government have a responsibility and a capacity to influence economic performance? We continue to struggle with these issues today.

Moral Dilemmas

1.   If, during periods of economic expansion, the government decreases spending and increases taxes, are the impacts or effects of these measures distributed equally among all subsets or segments of the population?

2.   Conversely, if, during periods of economic contraction, the government increases spending and decreases taxes, are the impacts or effects of these measures distributed equally among all subsets or segments of the population?

3.   Are there industries or firms that benefit from adverse business cycles?

4.   Are there industries or firms that are more harshly affected by adverse business cycles?

Moral Commentary

1.　　In a freely competitive market, when demand exceeds supply, there is a lag time before producers are able to increase output to match demand. Logically, in the interim, prices will rise. People with limited income may not be able to afford the price increase without sacrificing something else. Those with higher income may not be seriously affected. This may not create a problem with respect to luxury goods, but certainly will with respect to necessities. The question is, should producers benefit from the increase in profits, or should the government intervene through regulations, restrictions or other mechanisms? Should that intervention affect all goods or only necessities as opposed to luxury goods?

2.　　Keynes argued that consumption drives the economy, as opposed to investment, government or net exports. He ignored personal saving other than its role in providing funds for investment. What is the implication of this emphasis on consumption? Is this in the best interest of the consumer? As opposed to other industrialized countries, Germany and Japan for example, the historical personal savings rate in the United States has been very low; less than 1% of disposable income. People lack rainy-day funds, not to mention adequate funds for retirement. What, if anything, ought to be done to relieve this problem?

Chapter 3: Consumption and Saving

When you and I receive a paycheck, it is accompanied by a pay slip. That form tells us what our gross earnings were for the period and shows deductions such as withheld income taxes, and payroll taxes, such as Social Security and Medicare, and whatever benefit contributions have been withheld. The remainder is disposable income. We now face two choices: To spend or to save.

What you and I consume constitutes almost 72% of Gross Domestic Product (GDP). Total savings, which includes personal, corporate and government, accounts for 11% of GDP. GDP is a measure of the total amount of expenditures on final goods and services produced in the United States in one year. It is a vital measure of economic performance. Is the economy expanding, which is indicated by an increase in GDP? With the expansion, are there new employment opportunities? Are wages increasing? If the economy is not expanding, what can be done to reverse the trend? Because consumption constitutes such a large portion of GDP, the measures taken to reverse a negative trend have been to induce consumers to spend more.

What is consumption?

Consumption is the total amount that individuals spend on goods and services in the period of one year. The amount spent may be the result of income earned, of withdrawals from savings and investments, or from borrowed funds. All of which is to say that it is possible for individuals to spend more than they earn. In fact, in the years leading up to 2008, total consumption, the aggregate of all individual consumption, exceeded total earnings. The fact that consumers borrowed so heavily to maintain their level of living was one factor that led to the serious financial collapse and the great recession (sometimes referred to as the great contraction) of 2007 through 2009.

Consumption patterns have changed over the years. During WWII consumption was low because the war effort caused a reduction in production of consumer goods in order to maximize production of war material. In the period immediately succeeding WWII, families invested in homes, appliances and cars. As time and technology moved forward, spending patterns evolved to the point that today individuals and families spend 67% of their disposable income on services such as medical, education, and entertainment. The percentage of family income dedicated to food alone has dropped from 20% to 12% over a fifty-year period.

What is savings?

Some families set aside money to be saved before spending the remainder. Alas! They are the exception. Most people spend and then hope that something is left over to save. Regardless, savings are those funds that individuals and corporations do not spend. For individuals and families, savings may take the form of bank accounts, purchase of stocks and bonds, permanent or whole life insurance policies, or real estate, such as home ownership.

In fact, the illusion of constantly rising home values led people to borrow against the increase in equity, their share of ownership. This was done in the expectation that constantly rising home prices would enable them to repay their loans either from future income or the sale of the home. As a result of this behavior, when real estate prices fell, as they did in 2007 and 2008, and individual income declined, many families lost their homes to foreclosure. In a period when many Americans were dis-saving, that is spending more than they earned, there also were many individuals and corporations that continued to save. As you can imagine, the higher your income the greater likelihood that you will have funds to save, and the lower your income, the less the likelihood that you will be able to save.

As an industrialized nation, the U.S. has among the lowest savings rates in the world. Depending on economic circumstances, the rate of savings is not constant. For example, during the great depression the savings rate was negative. People were using every resource available to survive. During WWII, the savings rate was high because household incomes were increasing and there was little on which to spend money. Very few consumer goods, beyond essentials, were produced because of the war effort. In the post-war period, with significant pent-up demand, both incomes and savings were used to purchase homes, appliances and cars. It is, therefore, logical to think that the savings rate will increase during periods of prosperity and decrease during recessions.

However, in the period from 1980 through 2008, net disposable income did not increase for the middle class. This was the first time this phenomenon occurred in the post WWII era. As mentioned above, to increase their standards of living, households, particularly in the middle-income quartiles, reverted to extensive use of borrowed funds and to monetizing their home equity. When home values plummeted, the results were devastating to many typical American families.

What are the average propensity to consume (APC), and the average propensity to save (APS)?

It is one thing to know how much Americans spend or save from year-to-year. It is another thing altogether to estimate what an individual or consumer will do with an extra dollar earned. Business enterprises need to plan. They need to anticipate whether sales will be greater or lesser than the current period. In this context it is desirable to have information about what a consumer is likely to do, given a change in the level of disposable income.

Essentials of Macroeconomics

The average propensity to consume is the percent of disposable income individuals and households spend. The average propensity to save is the percent of disposable income individuals and households save. The two add to 1.0. The average propensities to consume and to save serve as base lines for the next concept.

$$APC = Consumption/Disposable\ Income$$

$$APS = Savings/Disposable\ Income$$

$$APC + APS = 1$$

The marginal propensity to consume is the percentage of change in the level of spending of disposable income.

$$MPC =$$

Percentage change in Consumption/Percentage change in Disposable Income

In most cases, it is logical to expect that those individuals or households earning higher levels of income will also have lower levels of a marginal propensity to Consume. That is to say, those with higher earnings will need to spend less of additional earnings to satisfy their needs and wants. As a consequence, individuals and households with higher levels of income ought to have the capacity to save a greater proportion of increased income. Their marginal propensity to consume ought to decrease.

Conversely, it is logical to expect that individuals who have low income, not only spend most or all of their income to satisfy their needs, but will likely continue to spend whatever increases in income they receive on necessities, as well; that is, their marginal propensity to consume ought to remain unchanged.

Theoretically, these concepts ought to reflect individual and household behavior. In fact, regardless of wealth, individuals and households have tended to spend or consume equally as high portions of their incomes to maintain or achieve higher levels of gratification.

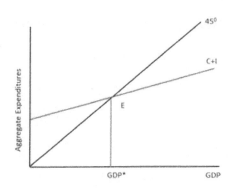

In the above graph, the 45° line represents equilibrium points where average expenditures equal GDP. Points to the left of the line indicate that expenditures exceed GDP, and to the right of the line, GDP exceeds expenditures. In either case the economy is out of balance. GDP* indicates equilibrium with consumption (C) and Investment (I).

What is the consumption function?

We are building a graph to demonstrate the relationship of consumption to disposable income and expenditures. The consumption function is that portion of total expenditures spent on goods and services by individuals and households. As disposable income increases the percentage of disposable income spent on goods and services is expected to decline.

In a graph, with disposable income on the "x" axis and expenditures on the "y" axis there is a line bifurcating the two at a 45° angle. If the same percent of disposable income is spent on expenditures, the intersection is on the line. If more disposable income is spent than there are expenditures the intersection is above the line. Likewise, if a less amount of disposable income is spent on expenditures, the intersection is below the line.

How can one spend more than one earns?

There are three ways to spend more than one earns:

1. Take money out of savings or investment accounts;
2. Borrow from banks or use credit cards which amounts must be repaid out of future earnings; or
3. Utilize government services, such as tax credits, food stamps, or a housing allowance.

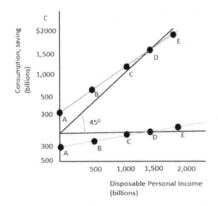

In the graph, if savings equaled disposable income, there would be no income for consumption. The yellow line indicates dissaving from points "A" through "D." On the green line, there are positive savings from points "A" through "D."

Essentials of Macroeconomics

What is the savings function?

If you recall, there are two options for the use of disposable income: To spend. To save. Consequently:

Disposable Income = Consumption + Savings.

On the same graph as above, the savings function is depicted as a line that reflects an increase in the marginal propensity to save. This is because, in most cases, it is logical that individuals and households which appreciate an increase in disposable income ought to be able to save an increasing portion of income received. If the level of the marginal propensity to save is less than disposable income, the intersection is to the left of the line, if it is greater than disposable income, it is to the right of the line. That is to say, an MPS to the left indicates negative saving or dis-saving. The importance of these relationships will become more apparent as we build the graph.

What is the difference between autonomous consumption and induced consumption?

Autonomous consumption is the amount of money people will spend on necessities, such as food, clothing and shelter, regardless of the level of income. It is referred to as autonomous because the amount of spending on necessities is relatively independent of changes in the level of disposable income.

On the other hand, induced spending is that amount spent on non-necessities, which very much depends on the level of disposable income. Induced spending is spending in response to gratification. It relates to individual aspirations and desires for a higher quality of life. It is logical to think that as disposable income rises, the percentage of disposable income spent autonomously is going to decrease and the percentage of induced spending is going to increase. Autonomous spending is related to satisfying basic human needs. The vast amount of advertising and promotions offered by corporations is to persuade consumers to increase their induced spending.

$$\text{Consumption} = \text{Autonomous Spending} + \text{Induced Spending}$$

What does the consumer buy?

Consumer buying is typically divided into three categories: Durables, such as homes, appliances, autos, items which tend to have a long life; nondurables, such as food and clothing, or perishable items that are readily consumed or have a short life; and Services, which are intangibles that have no shelf life and are either consumed or lost. Services include entertainment, restaurants, doctors, accountants and consultants.

Over time consumption patterns change. For example, fifty years ago the cost of food absorbed 20% of household income. Today only 12% of household income is spent on food. Fifty years ago, households spent 35% of income on services. Today, that number is 67%.

What determines the level of consumption?

There are seven factors that contribute to the level of consumption. They are:

1. Disposable income
2. Credit availability
3. Amount of liquid assets consumers have (savings and investments)
4. Amount of durable assets consumers have (appliances, autos, electronics)
5. Keeping up with the Joneses (putting on airs)
6. Consumer expectations (what is going to happen tomorrow?)
7. The wealth effect (the increase in value of assets owned)

Disposable income has already been explained. It is the net income after the deduction of income taxes, payroll taxes and other employee benefit costs. Some people restrict their spending to current income. Many people anticipate that their income will increase and adjust their current spending to expectations. Others are more cautious and deduct personal savings before determining disposable income.

Credit availability is the amount of money individuals and households are able to borrow to make purchases. Most homes in the U.S. are purchased with little equity (ownership, down payment) by the buyer. Rather, banks provide the majority of funds, up to 95%, required to purchase a home. Through lines of credit, home equity loans, auto loans, and credit cards, individuals and households are able to make current purchases and pay for them over time out of future income. As a percentage of total income, the amount of personal debt has increased substantially over the past 50 years.

Liquid assets are savings accounts and investments in stocks and bonds. All of these assets can be readily converted to cash, albeit in some cases at less than cost. Sometimes the accumulation of liquid assets leads consumers to overspend, thinking that they have more wealth than is truly the case.

Durable assets constituted major purchases immediately after WWII. Consumers swept up radios, phonographs, TVs, and washing machines. Later, these acquisitions were replaced by fancier sound equipment, hi-tech TVs, CD, DVDs, and more and more, as technology improved. Over time, the purchase of durable assets diminished as a portion of total consumption because demand was satisfied and durable assets had longer lives.

Are computers, laptops, tablets and cell phones durable goods?

From the point of view of durability or life expectancy, these goods are produced to last a number of years. On the other hand, producers intentionally design technological obsolescence into many products. By introducing new technology, innovations or features into subsequent products, manufacturers render the older models obsolete and create the desire for instant gratification in purchasing the newest model. Nevertheless, the product, technically, is durable.

Keeping up with the Joneses is an expression to describe avarice, which is the want of something because someone else has it. For good or for ill, much of the United States' consumption has been driven by subtle and not-so-subtle pressure to match one's neighbor's lifestyle. Ergo, the argument stated in the above paragraph.

Consumer expectations are the views people have about what may happen tomorrow. If consumers are uncertain about the future, it is logical for them to spend less and save more. In the same token, should consumers feel bright and confident about the future, it is likely that they will spend more and save less.

The Wealth Effect refers to the increase or appreciation of the market value of marketable assets. Because the increased value may be converted into cash, either by sale or by borrowing, consumers may directly benefit from the wealth effect by accumulating more assets or consuming more.

Milton Friedman originated the hypothesis of the permanent income effect. In essence, he argued that consumers develop a sense of what their lifetime average income is likely to be. On the basis of this, people generate consumption and savings patterns that fit this lifetime expectancy. This theory is useful in predicting general consumption and savings levels of the population.

Is the consumer really king or queen?

The answer to the above question is a resounding no. Over time, with the development of two income households, consumers actually have less flexible disposable income. The logic of this argument is based on the fact that families commit to certain lifestyles whereby they purchase homes, cars and levels of consumption that require constant maintenance. After paying a mortgage, taxes, insurance, auto loans, education costs and other on-going expenses, there is little flexible disposable income left.

Why do we spend so much and save so little?

This question is of particular importance since it largely explains the roots of the 2007 recession. Since the post WWII era, Americans have been ever increasing their levels of consumption. When real disposable income leveled off in the 1980s, Americans substituted savings with consumption to achieve gratification. The notion of saving before purchasing was replaced with acquire what you want today and pay for it tomorrow. This practice has been encouraged by both the public sector and the private sector. The government has made purchasing a home very inexpensive by effectively subsidizing mortgage interest rates. Banks and enterprises promote consumption.

What is total savings?

In this chapter we have discussed consumption. What is left of disposable income after deducting consumption is savings. In some households, consumption is what is left over after deducting savings. That is probably a more responsible use of disposable income. *Total savings* is the aggregate of all savings by individuals, families, corporations, and government.

When measuring GDP, consumption is the largest input. It constitutes about 72% of total GDP. Personal savings, on the other hand, until recent years, constituted about 5%. In the years leading up to the recession of 2007, personal savings actually became a negative number of -.5%. Since 2009, savings has once again become a positive number of about 4%.

Total savings is not just personal savings. It also includes business saving and government saving. In fact, total savings is now close to 11% of GDP. Because we rely on savings as a source of investment, it is essential that total savings be a strong, positive number.

How do corporations and government save?

When corporations generate more income than expenses, they produce profits. These profits may be paid out to shareholders in the form of dividends, used to repurchase company stock, retained for future growth and development or used to acquire other enterprises. If the proceeds are not used to expend plant and equipment, or build inventory, they will be used as savings to invest in equities or fixed income instruments. Additionally, companies may generate sales revenue more quickly than they incur expenses, and thus have extra cash to invest.

Governments may generate more revenue in the form of taxes and fees than the amount of their expenses and thus produce a surplus. This rarely happens, but as the federal government did between 1998 and 2000, there is an opportunity either to save or reduce debt. Also, in the same event as that applied to corporations, if the timing of the receipt of income is sooner than making payments to cover expenses, an opportunity to save, or invest occurs.

Summary

Consumption, as described in this chapter, is a driving force in the American economy. The essence of a free private enterprise system is to provide the goods and services demanded by consumers. What percentage of their disposable income is spent, and what portion of increased disposable income is spent, the marginal propensity to consume, is an important concept to help firms in determining what to produce and how much to produce. The health of the overall economy, GDP, is a reflection of consumer confidence, their demand to satisfy current and future wants, and their willingness to consume or to save.

Moral Dilemmas

1.   Is the level of consumption as a percent of GDP equally essential to economic prosperity and individual well -being? What would be the economic effect of an increase in savings at the expense of decreased consumption?

2.   What degree of personal responsibility do individual consumers bear if they fail to save adequately for medical emergencies, education, or retirement?

3.   What responsibility do producers bear for enticing consumers to spend more with low interest loans and generous repayment plans?

4.   What is it about human behavior that causes consumers to continue spending high percentages of their disposable income as that income increases?

5.   Do producers have a responsibility to ensure that all people have equal access to affordable durable products, services, and loans irrespective of level of income?

Moral Commentary

1.   For more than ten years, with the hope of stimulating investment, the Federal Reserve Bank has maintained a low interest policy. Not only does this policy affect interest rates in the bond market, and the level of commercial bank interest rates, it also affects consumer loans and personal savings rates. Individuals are discouraged from saving because the rates banks pay are very low, and, at the same time, because borrowing costs are low, individuals are

enticed to borrow and spend. How does this contrast with the expectation that humans will behave rationally, morally, and in their own best interests?

2.   Most industrialized countries that have a high level of personal savings have homogeneous populations. Does the fact that the U. S. population is very heterogenous have a significant influence over economic behavior with respect to both consumption and saving?

This topic will be addressed more in this book when we discuss the role of government and that of the Federal Reserve Bank.

Chapter 4: Investment

To understand the division of functions between the private sector and the public sector it is useful to understand two concepts: Rivalry and Excludability. Rivalry is the concept that not enough goods or services are produced to meet the total demand. Therefore, the goods or services one person obtains are denied to another. Excludability is the concept that unless one pays for the goods or services, one cannot obtain them.

The private sector engages in both rivalry and excludability. That is to say, that by intentionally not producing enough goods or services to meet total demand, firms are able to influence price. When there is greater demand than there is supply, prices increase. An increase in price creates more profits and motivates firms to produce more goods. To do so, firms must invest or inject financial capital to increase plant and equipment. If prices do not increase, or even worse decrease, then there is an indication that there is excess supply. This causes firms not to invest and, in some cases, to withdraw from the market.

What distinguishes firms from public sector entities?

Firms or enterprises are owned by individuals, not by the government. Firms in the U.S. have three forms: Proprietorships, Partnerships, and Corporations.

72% of business firms in the U.S. are proprietorships; yet, they produce only 5% of total output as measured in sales. Proprietorships are owned by one person, who is the owner/operator. Typical examples are retail stores, dry cleaners, auto repair shops, plumbing businesses, electricians, and other service entities.

Partnerships are firms owned by more than one person, who together are the owners/operators. Partnerships account for 9% of the total number of firms and produce 13% of total output. Partnerships are the preferred form of ownership among law firms, accounting firms and medical or dental practices.

Corporations are the most complex and fewest number of business firms, accounting for only 19% of total firms. Corporations, however, account for 82% of total output. Corporations are owned by shareholders, who are owners, but not operators.

Factor	Partnership	Proprietorship	Corporation
Ownership	Single	Multiple	Thousands
Management	Owner	Owners	Agent
Liability	Personal, extensive	Joint & several	Limited
Financial capital	Little	Modest	Vast
Organizational form	Simple	Relatively simple	Complex
Life	Mortality of owner	Mortality of owners	Perpetuity
Taxation	Personal	Personal	Direct to corporation

Because of their size, pervasiveness, overwhelming output and financial capitalization, the remainder of this chapter will be devoted to corporations. Corporations dominate almost every industry or productive sector in the economy: Exxon in the oil industry. Wal-Mart in retail sales. General Electric in jet engines, locomotives, appliances, health care equipment. Apple and Microsoft in technology. Archer Daniels in food commodities. Pfizer in pharmaceuticals, Amazon in internet sales, and so it goes.

Why do corporations so dominate the U.S. economy?

The answer lies in the vast amount of capital corporations require to produce highly sophisticated goods in huge quantities. Individuals and corporations are willing to invest their funds based on the fact that their liability to the corporation and its customers is limited to the amount of the investment and nothing more. Should the corporation need more capital to expand or to resolve liability disputes with customers, the shareholders cannot be held accountable or assessed for the amounts.

Corporations attract financial capital from three sources: Shareholders in the form of common or preferred stock. Bond holders in the form of debt instruments. Bankers in the form of short or long-term loans. In a sense all of these parties are investors, each with a different tolerance for risk and expectation of return. The shareholder of common stock, who also has the right to vote on corporate management and policies, expects a return in the form of dividends and appreciation of his/her investment. On the downside, the shareholder is willing to endure the volatility of the marketplace in determining share prices. The bondholder has no influence over management and expects a return on his/her investment in the form of a market rate of interest commensurate with the risk of the investment. The banker makes a choice between a short-term and long-term loan in expectation of an acceptable rate of return. The banker may exact covenants or conditions on a loan, giving him/her some influence over management, but not much.

Essentials of Macroeconomics

What is investment?

Investment is the use of financial capital to purchase plant, equipment, inventory and technology. When a corporation is formed, it attracts financial capital from its organizers and initial shareholders. As the corporation grows and expands, it frequently needs more capital than it generates from sales.

During normal times, investment in plant and equipment tends to be stable. There are three reasons for this phenomena: Investment in plant and equipment is long-term in nature, between planning and execution it is not unusual for five years to lapse. In the expansion phase of the business cycle, demand increases, prices increase and firms will increase equipment and technology. During recessionary phases of the business cycle interest rates may decline and firms, anticipating a reversal in the business cycle, may increase their borrowings to finance future expansion.

The elastic band or cushion for increase or decrease of capital is inventory. During expansionary periods, inventories decrease until firms have a chance to catch up with demand. As demand falters or the rate of increase in demand diminishes, inventories tend to increase. Firms slow down production to allow for inventory run-off, reflecting a decrease in investment.

The largest single factor in household expenditures is home ownership. The cost of purchasing, insuring, paying taxes on, and maintaining a home may reach as much as 40% of a household disposable income. This percentage is extremely high. The more typical household devotes about 30% to home ownership. The point is that the purchase of a home is very dependent on the cost of borrowing, i.e. the cost of home mortgages. When interest rates are high, purchases decrease. When interest rates are low, purchases increase. The planning and execution of home construction is generally medium-term in nature. There can develop inventories of unsold homes when interest rates unexpectedly take a turn for the worse, i.e. increase.

What is the relationship between savings and investment?

Investment funds are derived from funds saved. In Keynesian economics savings and investment are equated (savings = investment). This can be explained by an ordinary example of supply and demand. If savings are treated as the supply and investments are treated as demand, then each performs in its respective category. In the graph below, "D1" represents a level of investment demand whereby the quantity demanded increases as interest rates decline, and the increase is exclusively dependent on price (interest rates). "D2" represents a shift in investment demand based on other factors, such as changes in costs, increased need to build or replace plant and equipment, or acquisitions. In both cases, the supply of savings remains exclusively dependent on interest rates.

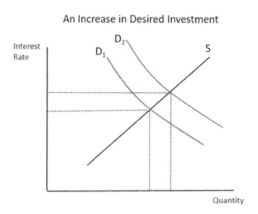

An Increase in Desired Investment

Individuals, firms and the government are all producers of savings funds. As such, they seek to maximize their return or profit. As prices or interest rates increase, more people, firms and government tend to increase their savings. As interest rates decline then so do savings, because the incentive to save has decreased.

What causes interest rates to rise or fall is the demand for those funds by investors (producers). Like consumers, investors look for opportunities to borrow at low prices or rates of interest, and their demand for funds decreases as the price or interest rates rise. An equilibrium is reached when both savers and investors agree on a price and quantity of funds that satisfies each. The equilibrium is reached by trial and error and, as in the case of general equilibrium, tends to be stable for a period of time.

There is a distinction between financial investments and "real "investment. Financial investment includes savings accounts, corporate stocks and bonds, and investment in government securities. These types of investments are an intermediary transaction that allows those who receive the investment to turn around and make real investments. That is, they take the funds and purchase land, plant, equipment, inventory and technology.

There is a difference between gross investment and net investment. That difference is called "depreciation." Depreciation may be defined as the cost incurred in the use of real investments. With the exception of land, all real investments, plant, inventory and technology either have limited usable life spans or their life is exhausted through use. To account for this expenditure, "depreciation" or a reduction in remaining value of plant, inventory and technology is applied. After deducting depreciation from gross investment, the result is net investment.

What determines the level of investment?

There are four factors that influence the level of investment. They are: Sales outlook; Capacity utilization rate; Interest rates; and Expected rate of return.

The sales outlook is a prediction of demand for goods. If, at the present level of production, inventory continues to decrease then the sales outlook is positive.

Essentials of Macroeconomics

Under such circumstances a firm might consider investing in more plant and equipment. If inventories begin to accumulate, that is an indication of over-production or that sales are declining. In such a scenario, no new investments will be made.

Capacity utilization rate refers to the level of output of a firm relative to its total potential output. It is normal for the current level of output to be less than 100% of total capacity. This permits time for maintenance and examination for potential breakdowns. If demand is increasing, even before full capacity utilization is reached, firms will determine whether or not to invest in additional plant and equipment.

Capacity utilization rate = current output/total potential output

Interest rates reflect the cost of financial capital. When interest rates are low, there is a high incentive to borrow funds to invest in plant and equipment. When interest rates are high, there is a high disincentive. Interest rates are inextricably interrelated with the expected rate of return. In effect, the higher the cost of financial capital, the more pressure there is to achieve a higher rate of return. It is for that reason that firms prefer to borrow long-term funds at low interest rates.

The expected rate of return is highly subjective and full of uncertainty. For one thing, there is a long lapse of time between the planning of an investment, its execution, and actual production. During this time, costs are accumulating without any return on the investment. Furthermore, demand may have decreased or new technology may make the product obsolete. For these reasons, the expected rate of return on a new investment is very high, ranging from 25% to 40%.

To the graph measuring consumption, we can now add the investment line. Points on the graph where consumption, and now consumption and investment are to the left of the 45° line indicates that, in this case, expenditures exceed both consumption and investments. As income and investment increase, they match expenditures upon intersecting with the 45° line. To the right consumption and investment exceed expenditures of GDP.

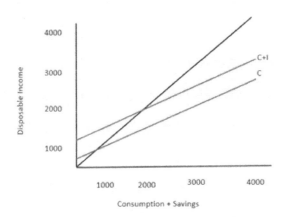

Summary

For an economy to prosper and reach its full potential there must be a balance between consumption and investment. If there is too much consumption and no savings set aside for investment, over time an economy will exhaust its plant and equipment and not be able to satisfy consumer demand, much less provide for additional population and increased demand. On the other hand, if consumption is too low, then the demand for goods and services will decrease and firms will reduce their investment in plant and equipment accordingly.

Moral Dilemmas

1.   Do all firms have equal or similar access to the supply of funds for investing?

2.   Should all firms have equal access?

Essentials of Macroeconomics

3.   Why might some firms be able to attract more funds at lower costs than others?

4.   What is the burden borne by firms that can only attract investment funds at high rates and in small amounts?

5.   What are the rewards of saving with respect to security, independence, and quality of life?

6.   What are the threats of not saving or failing to save enough?

7.   Do boards of directors and management have a moral responsibility to shareholders when choosing to borrow funds versus increase equity?

Moral Commentary

1.   The equilibrium interest rate for savings and investment represents what savers demand as suppliers of funds and what borrowers are willing to pay. Government actions also influence interest rates. For example, an increase in corporate taxes may reduce investment to expand output. Conversely, a reduction in taxes with the intention of motivating an increase in investment and subsequent increase in output, may not have the expected impact. The tax act of 2017 reduced corporate taxes from 35% to 21%. Contrary to expectations, the bulk of the savings were applied to repurchase of stock, acquisitions, and dividends. Only a small portion was used to expand output. The question arises, should government impose restrictions or limitations on the eligibility of reduced tax rates? Should corporations continue to be free to exercise individual judgement?

2.   Interest rates are also influenced by the Federal Reserve Bank (The Fed). Especially during periods or cycles of economic contraction, The Fed initiates actions to increase the money supply and thereby decrease interest rates. The

Essentials of Macroeconomics

purpose is to stimulate economic expansion by inducing both individual consumers and firms to borrow; the former to spend, and latter to invest. Left out in the cold are savers, particularly retired folks living on fixed incomes. The lower interest rates diminish their incomes disproportionately to the rest of the population. The question is, what role can the government play to rectify this unintended consequence?

Chapter 5: The Government Sector

We introduced the Saving-Investment sector by defining the private sector as one that engages in rivalry and excludability, as opposed to the public sector, which engages in non-rivalry and non-excludability.

You may recall that rivalry is defined as the consequence of one consumer acquiring a good or service and thereby depriving another consumer from acquiring that good or service. Excludability, on the other hand, is requiring consumers to pay a price to acquire a good or service.

How does the government or public sector differ from the private sector?

The government sector meets the demands of consumers by doing exactly the opposite. That is, the government sector engages in non-rivalry and non-excludability. The function of government is to provide sufficient goods and services to satisfy demand fully. Government also provides goods and services regardless of the consumer's ability to pay. These goods and services are provided for the good of the national interest, as well as to satisfy individual needs.

For example, it is for the common good that a national defense system be provided; that a fair and equitable judicial system is provided; that public safety in the form of police and fire protection is available to all; that universal education, at least K through 12 is available to all, and the list goes on.

Essentials of Macroeconomics

From the origins of the United States, when only bare minimal services were provided to today, federal, state, and local governments have substantially increased the size and scope of services rendered to the public. In the 18th century there was no national park system, there was no food and drug administration, there was no department of education and no social security or Medicare system. Generally speaking, the government has expanded to provide services to the public that the private sector was not willing to provide for lack of making a profit, or disinterest in providing a sufficient level of output to meet the entire demand.

With the growth of demand for public goods and government services, over time, it became readily apparent that governments at the federal, state, and local levels have an ever- increasing economic role.

What is the growing economic role of government?

Not until the great depression in the 1930s did leaders of business and industry and elected officials realize that the federal government could play a very important role in influencing economic expansion or contraction. Prior to 1929, reliable statistical information about economic activity was not available. Computing gross domestic product and its various components was done for the first time in 1934. In fits and starts during the great depression of the 1930s, the federal government injected new funds into the economy to foster public works and other forms of employment with hopes of reversing the economic slump and returning the country to prosperity. Only with the massive injection of financial capital to build military capacity to fight WWII did the great depression come to an end.

Today, the federal government expenditures account for 21% of GDP. Expenditures are divided into two categories: Entitlements and Discretionary. Entitlement programs are those long-term commitments created by the Congress, which require funding from year-to-year. They include Social Security, Medicare, net interest, and Medicaid. These entitlement programs account for 60% of the annual federal budget. With national defense, a non-entitlement program which enjoys near-entitlement status, the total rises to 80%. Discretionary expenses, which include the Departments of Justice, Commerce, Labor, Housing and Urban Affairs, Homeland Security and many regulatory and enforcement agencies, account for 20% of the federal budget. Discretionary expenses are subject to annual review and modification.

How does the federal government pay for the services rendered?

Sources of revenue to the federal government consist of federal income tax revenue (44%), Social Security, which is a transfer payment into the Social Security System (36%), corporate income taxes (12%), and other forms of revenue (8%). In recent times, the revenue shortfall has caused the federal government to borrow as much as 20% of the amount of the total budget to fund expenditures (deficits).

The nature of the lack of balance of the federal budget warrants some elaboration. An annual revenue shortfall, that is when expenses exceed revenue, creates a budget deficit. This deficit is funded by the issuance of debt instruments by the U.S Treasury. The accumulation of annual deficits constitutes the national debt. The national debt is funded by purchases of treasury obligations from the surplus in the Social Security System and sales of debt instruments to the public, both domestic and foreign.

There is always a national debate about the size and rate of increase in the national debt. It is rapidly approaching 100% of GDP. While there is no absolute or international standard of how much debt a country can sustain relative to its GDP, as the number increases it becomes increasingly a political hot button. The preoccupation about the size of the debt arises from a concern of how to repay it, and that the debt fuels inflation. Few citizens are willing to forego services or bear an increased share of the tax burden. The eventual solution to this problem is very difficult and has become an impossible conundrum to resolve.

How does state and local government spending differ from that of the federal government?

State and local governments focus on meeting the needs of their citizens that are not provided by the federal government. These needs are concentrated on education, general welfare, unemployment with federal assistance, and public works such as roads, highways, water and sewer systems and sanitation. Tax revenues are generated by sales taxes, real estate taxes, and in some cases, but not all, income taxes.

State and local governments are prohibited from funding general expenditures with debt. Consequently, annual budgets must be balanced. Only long-term investments in infrastructure or capital improvements may be funded by debt.

What are transfer payments?

Transfer payments are funds collected by the federal, state and local governments which are not used to purchase goods and services. They are funds which, once collected, go immediately to pay social security or similar benefits for which no work or value is expected. As such, transfer payments are excluded from government expenditures.

How is the government factor included in the calculation of GDP?

To total consumption and net investment, we now add government expenditures. The graph looks as follows:

$$GDP = C + I + G$$

As GDP increases, so do expenditures. Each incremental factor, consumption, plus investment, plus government adds capacity to GDP and consequently, expenditures.

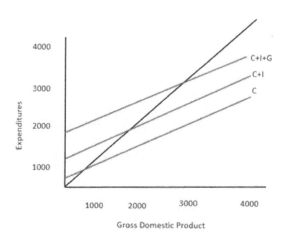

As the graph depicts, consumption, investment and government expenditures to the left of the 45° line represent spending in excess of the three factors. Expenditures to the right of the line are within disposable income ranges.

What are the various types of taxes?

Fundamentally, and in the final analysis, all taxes are born by the individual. Taxes do take different forms.

Direct taxes are those paid to a taxing authority by individuals or firms. They may take the form of an income tax or a payroll tax. Corporations pay income taxes, but in effect the source of that tax is revenue generated by sales to individuals.

Indirect taxes are collected by an intermediary, and take the form or a sales tax, real estate tax, or excise tax.

Essentials of Macroeconomics

Progressive taxes are those taxes borne disproportionately by higher income individuals over and above that of lower income individuals. Progressive tax is one of many forms of income redistribution. Federal income taxes are a typical example of a progressive tax.

Proportional taxes might also be called revenue neutral taxes. They are collected, irrespective of one's income level, at the same "fair" level from all individuals.

Regressive Taxes are those which have a tendency to impose a greater burden on the poor than on the rich. Social Security Taxes and sales taxes are examples of regressive taxes because they do not differentiate among poor and rich. All bear the same level of the tax burden. Because poor individuals have lower income, all of which is subject to social security tax deduction; and because lower income individuals spend a disproportionate amount of their income on goods and services, which are subject to sales taxes, these forms of taxation are considered to be regressive.

What are the sources of income to the federal government?

Let us discuss the sources of income to each level of government in greater detail.

The *personal income tax* generates 44% of total revenue to the federal government. It is a progressive tax because the level of tax or percentage of the income tax applied to income increases incrementally. Simply put, the tax at a low level of income is low as a percentage of income. As income increases, each additional or incremental amount is charged an increased level or percent of tax. This is known as the marginal tax rate. The average tax rate is computed by adding the weighted average of each of the marginal rates. The United States has one of the most complicated systems of income tax in the world. There are many deductions, too numerous to mention, such as charitable giving, interest and taxes paid on residential real estate, and capital gains taxes.

The *payroll tax* is a direct deduction from gross income, as is income tax. However, the amount of the deduction is fixed and relates directly to a benefit that the individual might receive at some time in the future, specifically, social security and Medicare or Medicaid.

Corporate income taxes are paid by corporations out of net profits. After deducting all expenses from gross revenues, the excess revenue over expenses is called profits. Producing profits is the fundamental objective of all corporations. After deducting taxes, corporations are then able to reinvest in their own enterprises, distribute income in the form of dividends to their shareholders, repurchase company stock, or a combination of the three.

Excise taxes are a form of sales tax. They differ from sales taxes in that they are a specific dollar amount and do not vary with the amount or price of a transaction. Goods subject to an excise tax have an inelastic demand curve (more on that later) such as cigarettes, liquor, and gasoline.

The estate tax, sometimes referred to as the death tax or inheritance tax, is a tax imposed on the assets of the deceased before the assets are passed on to survivors or beneficiaries. Over the years, varying amounts of minimal exemptions have been established, the current amount being $1 million.

The history of the income tax reflects both changing economic times and differences in objectives and policies of the two major political parties. For example, during the 1950s, the highest personal income tax marginal rate was 91%. (This rate applied only to annual earnings above $3,177,172). In 1981, under the Kemp-Roth Tax Cut the marginal rate was reduced to 50%. In 1986 the marginal rate was lowered to 28%. In 2001 and 2003, the relatively higher tax burden paid by high income individuals was further reduced, thus changing the progressive structure of the federal income tax.

Essentials of Macroeconomics

What are the sources of revenue to state and local governments?

The personal income tax is applied by about 1/3 of the states. The level of tax varies considerably and is contentious because there is evidence that higher income individuals seek to avoid residency in states with high income taxes.

The sales tax is the most common form of taxation at the state and local level. It is a percentage applied to the sales and, in some cases, use of goods and services in the state. Some states rely totally on sales tax revenue and some have none. The emergence of internet sales such as eBay and Amazon has created some controversy because such sales are not uniformly charged local sales taxes.

The property tax, or real estate tax, is applied against the assessed value of real estate property each year. It has become an essential source of revenue for municipalities and public educational districts.

What are the consequences of a multi-tiered tax structure?

During good times, when GDP is growing, most government entities are able to keep up with the growth and expansion of services demanded by the public. During the recession of 2007 to 2009, a serious contraction in federal revenue and spending placed a devastating burden on state and local governments. Not only did these governments face an increase in demand for services, such as unemployment compensation, medical care, and childcare, but their revenue sources diminished with no legal capacity to borrow funds to satisfy the demand.

How do taxes in the United States compare with those of other countries?

Such a comparison is really an apples and oranges comparison. One can look at the numbers and see, for example, that such countries as Sweden, Belgium and d France have tax rates in excess of 45%, while the U.S. and Japan are below 30%. What does this tell us? Nothing! The role of government and the spectrum of services provided by governments all over the world differ and reflect the values of people, societies and economies they serve.

What is the economic role of government in the United States?

As alluded to above, the role of government in each country should reflect the will of the people. In the United States those roles or functions include:

The provision of public goods and services fulfills the non-rivalry and non-excludability expectations of individuals. There are numerous goods and services which are required for the national interest without serving the profit motive that drives the private sector.

Redistribution of income has become one of the most controversial functions of the federal government in recent times. The prevailing believe that the poor should be attended by the rich and that some degree of redistribution of income is for the general welfare and to the benefit of the country as a whole has been a mainstay of the nation for generations. Whether these beliefs and policies endure or suffer significant restructuring remains to be seen.

Stabilization refers to the economic role of the government in stimulating growth and minimizing unemployment. This will be discussed at greater length in future chapters. Suffice it to say, the federal government is charged with taking measures to minimize over expansion of the economy and mitigate recession. This responsibility is primarily borne by the federal government and the Federal Reserve Bank.

Regulatory Standards and Enforcement has been an area of significant expansion in size and scope over the past fifty years. Some might date the increased role of a regulatory government back to the great depression and the introduction of the Federal Deposit Insurance Corporation and the Securities and Exchange

Commission. Over the intervening years governments have taken initiatives to affect workplace safety, pollution, product quality and safety, corporate governance, sales transactions and many other areas affecting public consumption and the environment.

Summary

From the time of the birth of our nation, when government services were minimal, to today when people impose a greater burden on governments to satisfy a wide variety of needs, the role of government has changed. That change is reflected in the number and scope of services rendered, in the form of taxable revenue generated to pay for those services and in the role the government plays as a partner with consumers, investors and the private sector in shaping and enhancing the U.S. economy. In addition to providing for a stable and equitable legal framework for free markets and private enterprise to thrive, the government also has a role to adapt to changing times and the needs of its constituents.

Moral Dilemmas:

1. What is the national goal of providing goods and services to people who do not pay for those benefits?

2. Does the reliance on real estate taxes to fund municipalities and public school systems provide sufficient resources to deliver fair, equitable, accessible and affordable services to a diverse population?

3. Is it the role of the federal government through a progressive tax system to influence income and wealth distribution or is the purpose to fund the federal budget by taxing the wealthy in greater amounts than those with lower incomes?

4. Should regulatory standards and enforcement, such as environmental, work-place safety, sanitary conditions, to name a few, be reduced and more reliance placed on individuals' and firms' initiative and responsibilities?

Moral Commentary

1.   There is no dispute regarding certain services provided by government: National defense. Judicial system, Public safety. Transportation infrastructure. Education. Veterans benefits. And to a lesser extent, social security. Who should determine other services: Public health. Nutritional meals. Housing. Environmental conservation. Income equality, Gun safety? Should the provision of any or all of these services be determined by elected officials or legislative referendums?

2.   An extension of the above question is that of how to pay for any and all government public goods and services? For example, social security is a transfer system whereby a flat tax, that is a fixed percentage of income known as a payroll tax, is imposed on all employees, up to a maximum income of $137,000 in 2020. The corporate tax rate in 2020 was a flat 21%; however, there are untold numbers of exclusions and exceptions which significantly reduce the tax burden to select industries and firms. Real estate taxes are a form of wealth tax. Should other assets which reflect accumulated wealth also be imposed? Is a progressive tax system fair and equitable, or should taxes be at the same rate for all individuals and firms (a flat tax system)?

Chapter 6: The Exports and Imports

On an absolute scale, because the United States is the world's largest economy, it is also the largest exporter and importer of goods and services. On a relative scale, the portion of the United States economy engaged in exports and imports is smaller than that of many other economies; Germany, the Netherlands, Japan, Taiwan, and South Korea to cite a few examples.

What is the importance and basis for international trade?

One could argue that no nation is totally self-reliant with respect to resources. On the other hand, one could cite any number of societies which have existed in a closed economy; that is one which does not exchange goods and services with other economic entities. In the former group are large nations with advanced industries or desires to become more developed, and reach a higher quality of life, such as Western European countries, the United States, Canada, Australia, and New Zealand. In the latter group are relatively under-developed or emerging nations, with low levels of advancement and, sometimes, little desire or ability to change, such as Russia, Cuba, and North Korea.

A fundamental reason for trade is to acquire foreign resources needed domestically to satisfy individual wants and needs. As a corollary to this demand, there is the existence of an abundance of resources to be developed and exported and thus generate purchasing power to import goods and services. In and of itself, there is an, albeit awkward, balance of those with abundance and those with scarcity, each of which can offset the other.

Out of this imbalance of resources emerges an opportunity to specialize. In economics, specialization is the ability to concentrate resources and energy to optimize production of a particular good or service. Specialization allows for competitive advantage to produce greater quantities of higher quality goods and services at lower costs.

Why does the United States have a negative balance of trade?
The balance of trade is the sum of exports less imports. When exports exceed imports the result is a balance of trade surplus. When imports exceed exports the result is a balance of trade deficit.

For twenty years after World War II the United States enjoyed a significant balance of trade surplus. The devastation of the industrialized nations of Europe and Asia created immense opportunities for United States' industry to export products throughout the globe. As those European and Asian economies restored their productive capacities, they emerged as strong competitors to United States' industries. They employed new plant and equipment, new technologies, and had lower labor costs. The demand for United States' products and services declined and/or met with increased competition. At the same time, the United States consumer was demanding more products at cheaper prices. In 1973, the Organization of Petroleum Export Countries (OPEC) reduced production of oil and contributed to a tripling of the cost of oil in the space of one year. Because the United States economy was heavily reliant on foreign sourced oil, it entered a period of continuous negative annual balances of trade.

Another post WWII phenomenon was the emergence of multinational corporations. These business firms, in addition to their domestic production facilities also built production plants located in or close to markets across the globe. Such plants permitted the corporations to be more competitive in local markets and to take advantage of local resources: Plant, equipment, natural resources, and labor. Over time, it became readily apparent that foreign manufacturing and service subsidiaries could also provide high quality and less costly goods and services for the United States market. Thus, developed the practice of outsourcing or off-shoring. While a great deal of attention is paid to the outsourcing of jobs to foreign locations, little attention is paid to those foreign corporations that outsource to the United States for the same economic advantages. The vulnerability of the United States labor market to outsourcing has been predicted to be limited to only about 10% of service jobs. On the other hand, the argument has also been advanced that any service that can be digitized can be outsourced.

The point should be made that factors other than out-sourcing or off-shoring have significantly affected the labor market in the United States, specifically technology, including the introduction and expansion of robot-technology.

How does the balance of trade affect gross domestic product?

Over the past few chapters, we have discussed consumption, savings and investment, and government expenditures as factors contributing to gross domestic product. As a factor of production, exports also contribute to gross domestic product. Goods and services which are produced in the United States and then exported to foreign countries represent additional final goods and services produced domestically. Imports are goods produced in foreign countries and therefore do not contribute to gross domestic product. Consequently, imports are subtracted from exports to derive a number called net export (Xn).

Gross Domestic Product (GDP) = Consumption (C) + Investment (I) = Government (G) + Net Exports (Xn)

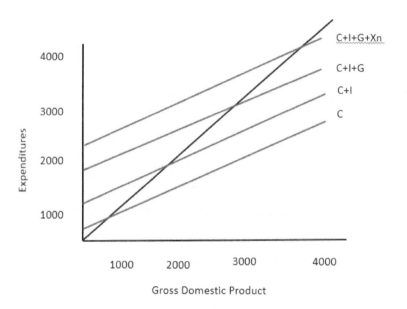

In the above chart, the final total measure of consumption (C), investment (I), government (G), net exports (Xn) is shown. The equilibrium is hypothetically set at $4 trillion GDP. To the left of the 45° bifurcating line, C + I + G + Xn (X) exceeds GDP. To the right the factors are less than GDP. The graph serves to point out that to the left, GDP is underperforming optimum potential and to the right, the reverse.

Should international trade be restricted?

There are a variety of tools available to restrict foreign trade. Generally, these tools are referred to as trade barriers. Nations have the right to protect their respective economies from foreign competition, should they choose to do so. Restrictions or barriers fall into three categories: (1) Tariffs, which are the equivalent of a tax imposed on imported goods, and therefore paid by consumers.

Examples are: computers, cell phones, footwear, and clothing; (2) Quotas, which are a numeric restriction on the quantity of a good permitted to enter a country. A primary example is sugar; and (3) Bureaucratic controls, which may take the form of standards of quality, processing requirements, or other forms of tedious paperwork. Examples are: agricultural products and pharmaceutical products.

An historic economic advantage held by the United States has been that of the world's largest common market. There are no trade barriers among the 50 United States. This enables immense economies of scale to meet the market demand of 125 million households or 328 million people. To emulate this economic advantage many nations have formed single trade areas or common markets.

The largest single trade area is the European Union. At last count, there are 27 countries with a population exceeding 420 million people in the Union. This Union was 60 years in the making and began as the European Steel and Coal Community in 1950. The Euro currency, which is used by 11 of the 27 countries, is the first step of a monetary union among European countries. The lowering of trade and monetary barriers has created significant trade opportunities for member nations and has also contributed to greater economies of scale and improved quality of life.

The North American Free Trade Association (NAFTA) now called The United States, Mexico, and Canada Agreement (USMCA) is a free trade zone created by the United States, Canada and Mexico. The imbalance of populations and purchasing powers make the United States by far the dominant partner in this association. Negotiations, which occurred during 2016 and 2017, preserve the free trade zone while modifying the terms and conditions under the agreement among the United States, Canada and Mexico.

The Central American Free Trade Association (CAFTA), and Mercosur, an association among Argentina, Brazil, Paraguay, Uruguay, and Venezuela are other attempts at creating economic opportunities through single trade areas. The associations have eliminated most internal trade barriers and erected common barriers against non-member countries. There are some persistent trade restrictions between Brazil and Argentina that have yet to be resolved.

Finally, on a global basis there have been many efforts to improve trade and reduce restrictions towards a goal of global free trade. The General Agreement on Tariffs and Trade (GATT) is the vehicle used for achieving this goal. GATT is administered by the World Trade Organization (WTO). Periodic negotiations among more than 150 nations have successfully reduced tariffs by 40%. Certain groups of products, such as agricultural products seem to elude success. Protection of intellectual property is also a sensitive issue, as is the issue of environmental protection. As one can imagine, the disparity of income and purchasing power among so many nations creates a very challenging environment in which to negotiate and reach equitable agreements.

Summary

The exchange of goods and services among global nations has generally been considered to be a major contributing factor to nations' economic development. While the U.S. exports and imports more goods and services in absolute numbers, the export-import sector of the U.S. economy is relatively smaller than that of nations such as Germany, Japan, or Korea. Prior to the 1970s the U.S. had a substantial trade surplus, only to lose that trade advantage to post WWII restored economies of Western Europe and Asia. Large single trade areas, emulating the massive market of the United States, emerged in Europe, Central and South America, some with greater or lesser success than others. To foment free trade and establish some common standards and practices, more than 150 countries have become signatories to the General Agreement on Tariffs and Trade (GATT).

Essentials of Macroeconomics

Moral Dilemmas

1.   Are the effects of outsourcing evenly and fairly distributed among industries, firms, and employees?

2.   If tariffs and other trade barriers protect industries, firms, and employees, what is the impact on consumers?

3.   Should trade barriers be used as policy weapons against countries deemed our adversaries?

4.   What roles does the consumer play in determining what goods and services to import and to export?

5.   Is it fair for importers to pass the cost of tariffs onto the consumer?

Moral Commentary

1.   Where the cost of labor is a prominent component of the production of goods or services, there is a significant incentive for firms to off-shore production of those outputs. If the purpose of an economy is to provide employment opportunities for workers, is this not contra-productive? Whose interests are being served, laborers, which represents 65% of the population, or consumers, which represents 100%of the population?

2.   There is no doubt that free and open international markets and international trade have an adverse impact on given national land, labor and capital resources. For example, in the United States entire industries have moved off-shore; textiles, electronics, and data collection and processing, to name a few. Some countries export their natural resources: copper from Chile, Tin from Bolivia, Bauxite from the Dominican Republic. Gold and diamonds form various African nations as examples. These resources suffer from depletion and are

irreplaceable. What measures should those nations take to preserve those resources or find alternative means of building and sustaining their economies? For example, recognizing that its oil reserves are being depleted, Dubai, one of United Arab Emirates, has developed an intensive service and hospitality industry. Should the nations or firms benefiting from the utilization of those resources bear some responsibility to provide for the future well-being of the exporting countries?

3.   The United States in the process of producing large quantities of good, generates large quantities of waste (unintended consequence, spillover). Should the United States dispose of its own waste or is it morally responsible to export waste to other countries?

Chapter 7: Supply and Demand

What is consumer demand?

Let's begin with a real-life event. In April 2010 the makers and distributors of 3-D movies decided to increase the price of admission of $9.60 to $11.80, an increase of 23%. After all, they had the only 3-D movies to see. As a result, total revenues declined 16%. What happened? Why did total revenues decline instead of increase? The answer lies in the price elasticity of demand. Had the makers and distributors understood this important concept, they would have decreased the price rather than increased it. What they failed to understand was that the issue was not demand for 3-D movies. The issue was demand for general entertainment. What other options did consumers have on which to satisfy their demand to be entertained? The options ranged from other movies, live entertainment, DVDs, program television, and on and on.

Consumer demand may be defined as an individual want or desire for a product or service, or an aggregation of all individuals, representing the sum of the entire population's wants or desires. In every stage of life, we are all consumers. It begins with basic wants of food, clothing and shelter and from there it increases with income to wanting more of everything from basics to luxury goods and services. As consumers, our ability to satisfy our wants is heavily influenced by prices of the costs of goods and services.

What is producer supply?

In the discussion about demand, you were wearing the hat of a consumer. All explanations of demand are focused on the rational behavior of consumers. Take your consumer hat off. You are now engaged in a discussion of supply. Put your producer hat on. Supply is governed by the behavior of producers and producers are focused on maximizing profits.

Producers do not manufacture or produce goods and services arbitrarily. Producers respond to consumer wants, both present and future. Goods and services can only be sold if they are desired by consumers. Therefore, supply reflects the quantity of goods and services producers are willing to make available to the market in a given time and at various price levels.

What is the relationship between prices paid and the quantity demanded by consumers?

The relationship between price and quantity demanded is inverse or negative. With rare exceptions, an increase in price will cause or result in a decrease in quantity demanded by consumers. Likewise, a decrease in price is likely to cause or generate an increase in quantity demanded by consumers.

What is price elasticity of demand and how is it measured?

Demand is measured in terms of prices and quantities. Until producers become aware of the quantity of their products in demand, they generally produce a limited amount. If consumers demand more of the product in the short run, producers will respond to the increase in demand with price increases. If the increase in demand persists, producers will increase the supply. Once the level of demand is satisfied, prices taper off or decrease to former levels.

This adjustment is not easy or smooth. At a given level, the demand for a product might increase. Because there are limited amounts of the product available, the price of the product will increase. With the increase in price, the demand may decrease. In the meantime, the producer is busy making more products. By the time that additional quantity of product reaches the market, the level of demand may have declined, in which case, the producer has to lower the price to stimulate more demand.

The point of this exercise is to state that both price and quantity change dynamically in a freely competitive market. Economists measure this dynamic change in terms of price elasticity of demand. Price elasticity of demand is quantifiably measured by comparing the percentage change in quantity consumed against the percentage change in the price of the product.

What are the differences between inelastic, unitary and elastic prices?

Inelastic price elasticity of demand is defined as a one percent change in price that will result in a less than one percent change in the quantity sold (demanded). Basically, what we are saying is that consumers are relatively insensitive to a change in price. This is usually the case because the product is so important or essential to the consumer that he/she must have it regardless of an increase in price. Likewise, the consumer is unlikely to increase purchases of the good or service just because the price decreased. The results of a one percent increase in price of a product with an inelastic demand will be an increase in total revenue, which is the sum of price times the total quantity sold. Graphically, a price inelastic demand looks like this.

Inelastic Demand

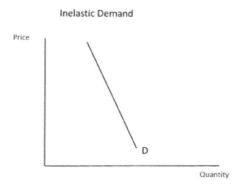

Unitary price elasticity of demand is defined as a one percent change in price that will result in a one percent change in quantity sold (demanded). The results of a one percent change in price of a product with a unitary demand will be an equal change in total revenue. Graphically, a price unitary-elastic demand looks like this:

Unitary Elasticity

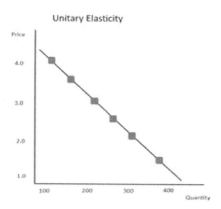

Elastic price elasticity of demand is defined as a one percent change in price that will result in a greater than one percent change in quantity sold (demanded). What this means is that consumers are relatively sensitive to changes in price. Usually price elastic goods are luxury goods with which consumers can do without. If the price increases there will be a decrease in quantity demanded. If the prices decrease, quantity demanded will increase. The results of a one percent change

Essentials of Macroeconomics

in price of a good or service that has an elastic price elasticity of demand will be a decrease in total revenue. Graphically, an elastic price elasticity of demand looks like this:

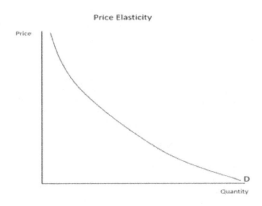

Price Elasticity

To be observed in the above diagram is the fact that to the far upper left the curve starts out as inelastic. As one moves down and to the right, elasticity of demand gradually increases, until one arrives at the far right where demand elasticity is perfect; that is, price stretches out infinitely.

A couple of facts to be kept in mind are: 1. As stated earlier, the relationship of price to quantity is inverse; that is to say, when the price of a product changes, increases or decreases, the quantity demanded changes in the opposite direction. A price increase will generate a lower quantity sold. A price decrease will generate an increase in sales. 2. For the sake of simplicity, when economists refer to movement on a single line, they are addressing exclusively the consumer response to a change in price. Do you recall the expression "all other things being equal"? This is exactly the point. The issue is one of isolating the price factor in order to explain human economic behavior exclusively in respect to price.

Essentials of Macroeconomics

What other factors affect elasticity of demand?

We concluded the above discussion by saying that movement on a single line measured exclusively the consumer response to a change in price. Other factors also impact consumer demand. Those factors include changes in: Taste. Disposable income. Population. Prices of other goods. and Expectations. These changes affecting the demand for goods and services are explained graphically by shifts in the demand curve.

Taste is a word used to describe consumer's response to new technology, changes in style or fads, and to competition, and a world of product differentiation. For example, as people become more environmentally conscientious, there is a shift in demand for cars that consume less gasoline per mile. Graphically, this shift in demand would appear as follows:

If the original price elasticity of demand is determined to be inelastic, the line reflecting the shift in demand will likely be inelastic as well. Likewise, if the original demand curve is elastic, the resulting shift will also be elastic.

Over the past thirty years middle income Americans have seen relatively little increase in disposable income. Two important factors have contributed to an increase in demand for goods and services. They are: Increases in population and increases in consumer debt. Without enjoying the benefit of increased disposable income, consumers borrowed money to acquire more goods and services. Finally, households live within budget and borrowing constraints. Wants and desires can be satisfied only if prices of all goods remain stable relative to one another. In the real world such is not the case. Prices of differing goods and services are constantly changing. If the price of seafood increases, it is likely that the consumer will decrease purchases of seafood and purchase poultry or meat. When the price of fuel escalates the demand for air travel and hotels diminishes. The converse is also true.

How is price elasticity of supply measured?

You have just removed your consumer's hat and donned the hat of a producer. Increases in prices motivate you to produce more. The first factor to keep in mind is that the relationship of price to quantity on a supply curve is direct. That is to say, that as price increases, a producer will increase the quantity produced. That is because higher prices lead to higher profits.

Elasticity of supply curves vary reflecting the underlying costs of the goods or services produced. As in the case of the demand curve, a movement along the line of a supply curve indicates exclusively a response to a change in price. As in the case of the demand curve, the supply curve may shift, as well. A shift in the supply curve reflects changes in several factors: A change in the cost of raw materials. A change in technology. A change in the number of suppliers (competitors). A change in the prices of other goods produced. A change in the prices of complementary goods and expected future prices.

What is a complementary good?

Some goods and services are typically accompanied by another good. For example, the demand for hotdogs also affects the demand for hotdog buns and mustard. The demand for cars affects the demand for gas, tires, and repair services. The demand for smartphones affects the demand for WiFi and streaming services.

What is the relationship between demand and supply?

When placed on the same graph, the demand curve and the supply curve will intersect. This point of intersection is called an equilibrium point. It represents the combination of price and quantity that will satisfy both consumers and producers. It is not achieved by mathematical calculation, but rather by trial and error. In the real world both demand and supply fluctuate over time and from market to market. Once equilibrium has been reached, however, there tends to be little change or more stability in both price and quantity.

What is consumer surplus?

A consumer surplus occurs when the market price paid by consumers is lower than the price they might be willing to pay. If there is a high demand for a product and a low supply, consumers, in competing with each other to obtain the product, will drive the price up. This will cause an increase in the consumer surplus. Conversely, with high prices, producers will likely increase production (supply) which should have the effect of lowering prices. Consequently, the consumer surplus will decrease.

The importance of the concept of consumer surplus is that it measures how efficiently a competitive market satisfies consumers' wants. The lower the price consumers pay and producers accept, the greater the satisfaction or well-being of consumers.

What is producers' surplus?

A producer surplus occurs when the market price charged by a producer exceeds his/her costs or what price they might be willing to sell the good or service. At any given level of demand, a certain number of producers will offer their goods and services. If the consumer demand drives the price upwards, so that it achieves a price level above and beyond what the producer would be willing to charge, a producer's surplus is created. As demand decreases, or supply increases, market prices will likely decrease and thus reduce the producer surplus. Likewise, should consumer demand remain unchanged and the number of producers (supply) decrease, prices will likely increase and so will the producer surplus.

Total Surplus

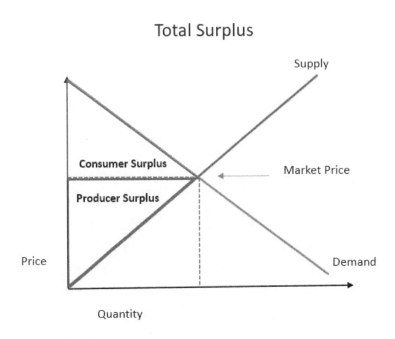

The importance of the concept of producer surplus is that it measures how efficiently a competitive market satisfies producers' wants. The higher the price consumers pay and producers receive, the greater the satisfaction or well-being of producers.

What are price ceilings and price floors?

From time to time governments decide to intervene in markets to influence prices. For example, in times of war, governments have restricted production of consumer goods and services to redeploy productive capacity to war materials. Other examples are price ceilings whereby an upper limit for prices is established, and price floors, whereby minimum prices are established. Governments have intervened in markets to protect consumers against escalating farm prices by imposing ceilings on such prices. Rent control is another form of a price ceiling. Ceilings are imposed when the supply is insufficient to meet demand, causing prices to increase beyond consumers' ability to pay.

Similarly, the establishment of a minimum wage is, in effect, an intervention in the market to impose a wage floor. As opposed to a price ceiling, the floor is established because there is a surplus causing prices, in this case wages, to decrease.

What is the rationing function of the price system?

Under the free market system, the rationing function of prices is perhaps the most important function of prices. Direct demand is the consumer demand for final goods and services. Demand for the inputs, land, labor, and capital, is defined as indirect demand. If the demand of a final product increases, then the demand for the resources required to make that product will rise as well. Applying the concept of the production possibilities curve, the increase in demand for an input, will necessarily deprive another user from access to that input. Conversely, if the demand for a final product decreases, then the demand for the input will decrease as well, thus making the input cheaper and more accessible to another application or use. The consequence of an increase in demand is an increase in price for the input. The consequence of a decrease in demand for the input is a decrease in price. Thus, the price function serves as a mechanism to determine the allocation of resources.

Summary

Firms make decisions about what products to produce and what quantity to produce based on consumer demand. Some products are relatively insensitive to changes in price, inelastic demand, and some products are very sensitive to changes in price, elastic demand. In addition, producers are constantly searching for the least expensive manner in which to provide a product or service. This involves exploring the use of different inputs, applying new technology, observing competition and the costs of other goods.

If the equilibrium price increases, there is an opportunity for increased profits, increased output and new competition. If the equilibrium price decreases, profit opportunities diminish and the number of suppliers, competitors, decreases as well. This process, which might be defined as the survival of the fittest, demonstrates how the price function serves to determine the allocation of resources.

Moral Dilemmas

1.   Are markets sufficiently efficient to assure affordability and accessibility to goods and services by individuals and families of all income levels?

2.   Do producer surpluses motivate producers to decrease supply and thereby increase profits? If so, how is the resulting increase in prices likely to impact consumers?

Moral Commentary

1.   The explanation of the relationship between supply and demand hypothetically assumes a perfectly competitive market. In fact, most markets are not perfectly competitive, but rather represent proportionately dominant competitors controlling greater than 60% of the market of any given good or service. Some examples are PC operating systems, cable television providers,

cell phones, chicken, breakfast cereals, etc. In addition to facilitating economies of scale, this also enables greater influence over price by limiting supply. What measures, if any, should be taken to maintain competition and optimize accessibility and affordability?

2.   Theoretically, the excess profits generated by industry concentration should do one of two things: 1. Motivate suppliers to increase output, or 2. Attract new entrants to the market. In the meantime, suppliers continue to generate excess profits at the expense of the consumer. Is the value of maintaining the principle of free and open markets sufficient to avoid market intervention and the resulting consequences on those who lack accessibility and affordability?

Chapter 8: Resource Allocation

Economics may be defined as the study of the optimal use of scarce resources to maximize the satisfaction of the insatiable wants and needs of consumers. The key words are <u>scarcity</u> and <u>insatiable</u>.

What are the implications of scarcity and insatiable?

It is difficult to understand the importance of studying economic principles and concepts without first appreciating the meaning of scarcity and insatiability. As one observes the world about us, it appears that resources such as air and water are abundant and cheap. However, if you then apply the adjectives clean and pure, these otherwise abundant resources all of a sudden become both scarce and expensive.

Likewise, one might observe that most people are able to live very simply and inexpensively. Nevertheless, once again, if you add the factors of affluence and greed, then many people's level of needs and wants constantly increase and are never fully satisfied. The central problem to economics then becomes, "How do you satisfy insatiable needs and wants given scarce resources?"

What are resources?

In economics, we refer to three principle resources: Land, Labor, and Capital. Recently, some economists have added entrepreneurial skill. By land, we mean all of the natural resources such as air, water, soil, minerals and land contents. By labor, we mean the world's population with all of our varying degrees of skills, or lack thereof. The labor force consists of physically and mentally able people between the ages of sixteen and sixty-five. By capital, we mean plant and equipment. Please note that in economics money is a form of financial capital, not economic capital.

What is land utilization?

Land mass of a particular country is divided between that which is arable, that is, suitable for growing crops, and that which is not. For example, 17% of land in the United States is arable. In the Peoples' Republic of China, the comparable amount is 13%. Beyond the measure of arable land, there are the measures of the amount of fresh water, and the amount and variety of mineral content, while also taking into consideration the factors of accessibility and affordability to exploit. Land utilization reflects the type of use. For example, is land used for agriculture, mining, water for drinking and irrigation, or development for housing, factories, retail malls or public services? Of total land available, what percent is used?

What is labor utilization?

Not all those people who meet the definition of eligible members of the labor force are fully engaged in productive activities. Labor utilization is measured by the labor force participation rate; that is, the number of those who are eligible and actually working divided by the total labor force. In the United States in 2019 the participation rate was 63%. Even that number is imprecise because it fails to distinguish among those who are under-employed; that is working in an activity that does not fully utilize their skills, or those working part-time.

What is capital utilization?

Keep in mind that capital refers to plant and equipment. The aggregate or total sum of all plant and equipment in the economy dedicated to the production of outputs requires other inputs or resources to optimize production. Theoretically, there is a quantity of output that the combination of physical capital, plant and equipment, can produce at its optimum level. That quantity of output represents 100% capacity utilization. Any output level that is less than the optimum is a measure of capacity utilization of less than 100%.

Do all resources produce the same results?

Do they yield the same benefit? Are some resources more suitable for certain applications than for others? The answer to those questions lies in the concept of opportunity cost. An opportunity cost may be defined as the next best use of a resource to that of its present application. If I am working as a college professor, given the education and experience that I have, would my talents be more effectively used in the finance profession? The answer to that question in economic terms, and as measured by income, would indicate that I should employ my talents in finance, not teaching. Note that I mentioned "in economic terms." The study of economics frequently, but not always, ignores human values and other unquantifiable factors.

At any given point in time, economists assume that all available resources are known and quantifiable. This assumption is important because it enables the discussion of whether or not an economy is operating at the maximum potential of the combination of all of its resources. The goal or objective of any economy is to realize the full potential or optimal utilization of the use of its resources. That is measured by reaching: Full use of available land resources. Full employment, frequently measured as unemployment of no more that 4% of the workforce (as an aside, only unemployed individuals who are actively seeking new employment are considered to be unemployed) and full production, frequently measured as 90% capital utilization. Note that neither level is 100%. That is because there are always shifts and adjustments making it both unlikely and unrealistic to expect 100% or full employment, and 100% capacity utilization. Sufficient excess capacity enables the economy to avoid scarcity and price inflation. Full use of land resources is a complex factor because pure air and pure water may be difficult to measure, while the amount of arable land is quite specific, as are available land resources.

Why is this chapter entitled Resource Allocation?

By allocating resources to particular functions, people are managing those resources with the expectation of optimizing their utilization or achieving the best and highest use of the resource. In the past, this has largely been a trial and error process. With the advent of modern technology, not to mention artificial intelligence, the trial and error process has been replaced with simulations and virtual applications.

How then is the allocation of resources determined?

Resources are allocated in response to the demands of people to satisfy their wants. A corollary to full use of all available resources is that not all wants will be satisfied. Consequently, there is a constant struggle or competition to reallocate the use of resources from production of one item to another. This discussion evolves about the concept to the production possibilities frontier curve.

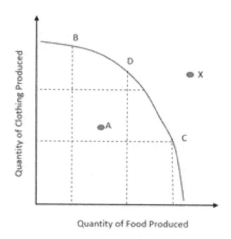

Production Possibilities Frontier Curve

Essentials of Macroeconomics

What is the production possibilities frontier curve?

Essential to the concept of the production possibilities curve is the law of scarcity. That is, given the amount of resources, more of one good cannot be produced without decreasing the amount of resources allocated to the other good. I like to use the example of food and clothing. It is graphic in many ways. If fifty percent of resources are allocated to each of food and clothing, the population (consumer) may be fully satisfied. If 100% were allocated to food then we would all run around naked. That is just fine in the heart of the Amazon jungle, not Cleveland, Ohio. On the other hand, if 100% of resources were allocated to clothing, we would all starve to death. Somewhere in between there is a happy medium.

The curve itself is called the production possibilities frontier, as that is the attainable production level given the currently available amount or resources. While this zero-sum game theory may appear arbitrary and unrealistic, it does serve to point out that increasing the consumption of one item, by definition requires the sacrifice of the consumption of a second item. If total production or output falls below the frontier, then there is an underutilization of resources. If through either a temporary blimp or the application of new technologies, output surpasses the frontier, then the level of full production has increased and a new frontier has been created.

How is the use of a resource measured?

The use of resources is measured in costs per unit of output. Those costs to the producer convert to prices for the consumer. There are two factors that determine the allocation of resources. First, if costs per unit of input increase, causing the price of the output or product to increase for the consumer, then the consumer has a choice of paying the higher price or not purchasing the good. If the consumer opts to continue buying the product then production will increase and more resources will be applied to production of that particular good. If consumers determine not to purchase the product because of the higher price, the production will decrease and the resources required will be reallocated to another use.

Secondly, if demand for the product is reduced because the product has become obsolete or replaced by a new invention or innovation, then the resources used as inputs for the formerly demanded product will decrease. The opportunity cost for using those resources has increased making its cost unjustifiable. All of which is to say that cost factors of production seek the highest level of efficiency, or in other terms, the least cost level of production.

Summary

Economic resources are land, labor, and capital, the latter being defined as plant and equipment (to include technology). Each resource is measured on the basis of utilization to determine if the resource is being applied to its optimum use, that being for the maximum benefit for the society it serves. Not all resources produce the same results nor yield the same benefit. Given a production frontier, that is the optimum potential of an economy, the production possibilities curve demonstrates that changes in the output of one good, necessarily impacts the output of another good (increase or decrease). The unit costs of inputs and the use of resources affect the ultimate price of the final good, which consumers may choose to purchase or not. In this context, the prices of final goods affect what and what quantity of goods producers will make. The allocation of resources to achieve their highest and best use is a function of the price mechanism.

Moral Dilemmas

1. Should the price mechanism be the sole factor in determining the allocation of a resource? How else might the allocation of a limited or scarce resource be determined?

2. With portions of the population lacking in basic necessities such as food, clothing and shelter, should resources be dedicated to producing what might be characterized as frivolous goods and services to satisfy a more affluent population instead of providing the basic necessities?

3. How might indirect costs such as environmental pollution be built into production costs?

Moral Commentary

1. With only 5% of global population, the United States consumes 25% of global raw materials. Given the percent of global population living at or near the poverty line, is this fair and equitable? Furthermore, with the rise of emerging nations such as China, India, and Brazil, the demand for these "precious" resources will inevitably increase. Can this competition be resolved amicably?

2. Some resources are scarcer than others. Likewise, some products utilize a disproportionate amount of a given resource. Some examples are: aluminum for aircraft. Rare earth for computers and cell phones. Lithium for rechargeable batteries. Should use of such scarce resources be rationed, regulated or otherwise governed for present and future generations? Are these resources being used for their respective highest and best use?

Chapter 9: Economic Growth and Productivity

What is economic growth and how does it occur?

The size of an economy is measured by the sum or total value of final goods and services produced by an economy in one year. Economic growth is an increase in total output of final goods and services. It is achieved either by applying an increased amount of resources to production, or by introducing new technologies or efficiencies, such as better trained workers, automation and technological innovation. Growth in a nation's economy is an essential objective.

Why is economic growth so important?

Think about what the world would be like if there were no economic growth to serve increasing levels of population. Remember, the U.S. had a population of 123 million at the time of the Great Depression in 1930. Without economic growth, how would today's population of 328 million survive? Furthermore, without economic growth, how would the quality of life or the standard of living improve? For these reasons, all nations seek to achieve economic growth. Indeed, in countries such as China and India, 9 and 10% rates of growth have been typical over the last ten years, while that of the United States has hovered closer to 3% per annum. The coronavirus of 2020 heavily influenced the above performance.

How does one understand statistical comparisons?

This is a good time to introduce a note of caution about interpreting statistical information. Keep in mind that the formula for the rate of growth is: (GDP2 – GDP1)/GDP1. If the numerator has a large change and the denominator is small, then the rate of growth will be high; however, if the numerator in two different examples is the same amount, but the denominator is large, then the rate of change will be smaller. As a case in point, if China, India and the United States had the same absolute amount of growth in GDP, but China and India had smaller base years, the China and India percentage rates of increase would be significantly higher.

Let us reiterate the points made thus far in this chapter. We have stated that it is a goal of every nation to achieve economic growth. Growth is measured by an increase in Gross Domestic Product. Economic growth can be achieved in three ways:

- Adding resources to increase output.
- Increasing efficiency by combining resources at the lowest level of cost.
- Introducing new technology and innovation.

Where resources (land, labor and capital) are limited, then increasing the output of one product necessarily requires the decrease of production of another product. This was demonstrated in the production possibilities curve. When an input or resource is underutilized, the opportunity cost, or next best use of the resource, demonstrates that the resource should be transferred to another application. Emphasizing economic growth has long been a policy objective of the federal government and the Federal Reserve Bank.

What impact did the industrial revolution have on American economic development?

The industrial revolution was marked by the invention of the first practical functioning steam engine by James Watt in 1765. This historic event enabled economies to change radically from largely agrarian economies, with urban concentrations of manual labor, to economies of mass production, thus facilitating the growth of a middle class and providing significant improvements in the quality of life. The change did not occur overnight. In England, where James Watt lived, it took 58 years to double per capita GDP. From the beginning of the Civil War in the U.S., it took 47 years to double per capita GDP. Now, per capita GDP in the US doubles about every 25 years. Expressed in different terms, that is a compound annual growth rate of 2.8%. Unfortunately, statistics reveal monetary increases but not improvements in the standard of living.

The industrial revolution has been characterized as having three phases:

- Phase one was marked by the introduction of the factory system, by smelting iron to create steel, and by the development of an extensive railroad system. (Marked by early 19th century to 1900)
- Phase two saw the mass production of cars, an electrification of the country, the use of electric machinery, production of steel, oil, and chemicals, and diminished reliance on hydroelectric power. (Marked by 1900 through post WWII)
- Phase three brought the introduction of consumer electronics, computer and communication systems, and manufacturing process innovation. (Marked by 1950 through 1970).

A new revolution commenced with the advances of computer technology.

- We refer to this stage of economic development as the information age

- Cyber technology is an extension of the information age.

What is productivity?

Let us begin this discussion with a definition of production, which is a measure of total output. Literally, production means "the act of producing." Productivity is a measure of the change in output relative to the factors of production or inputs. For example, if it takes fewer workers to produce a good, then productivity of labor has increased. Likewise, if a good can be manufactured using fewer raw materials, such as steel or aluminum, productivity of resources (land) has increased. On the other hand, if the cost of an input increases, such as an increase in wages, or the price of steel, then productivity will be negatively affected, or decrease.

What are the causes and benefits of increases in productivity?

Another way to define productivity is as a measure of output per unit of input. When output increases at a rate slower than the increase of inputs, it is called diminishing returns. When output increases at a rate greater than the increase in inputs, it is called economies of scale. Obviously, the latter is preferable to the former. From a human capital point of view, it is desirable that more output results from fewer hours of input of labor. This is the essential justification for an increase in hourly wages, or conversely, without an increase in productivity of labor, it is difficult to justify increases in wages.

Savings and investment affect growth in productivity because without savings and investment, neither new resources can be brought into production, nor can new technology be developed and introduced. In prior chapters, we have discussed the role of savings and investment. For purposes of this discussion, it is important to note that during the first decade of the 21st century, personal savings became negative or, to put it another way, consumers were spending more than they earned. This negative savings rate placed added pressure on the economy because it is from savings that investments flow into the economy. To make up for this shortfall, the U.S. has depended on investment funds from corporate savings and foreign sources.

Does an increase in the financing of the national debt affect domestic investment?

Another factor that has been thought to hinder the growth of domestic investment has been the increase in the national debt. As annual deficits have increased, the United States government has had to enter the bond markets to fund those deficits. This is an example of the "crowding-out effect," which occurs if the size of financial capital markets is limited. It also serves to point out the increasing reliance on global financial markets to meet the demand for investment funds. Thus far, even with substantial increases in the United States national debt, private enterprises have not encountered difficulty in funding debt. Bear in mind that investments made to replace depreciated plant and equipment and/or to replace depleted land resources only allow the economy to remain at the same level of productivity. Net new investments contribute to an increase in national output and productivity.

What is the role of labor with respect to changes in productivity?

Changes in the labor force have affected productivity. At the beginning of the 20th century, the average work week was 60 hours. Since 1990, the average work week has not varied significantly from 34 hours. Yet, during that period, the annual increase in productivity averaged about 2.3%. Since 2008, U.S firms have learned how to produce more with less labor. At a level of 5.8 million people, almost 3.6% of the labor force (160 million) is unemployed, excluding the coronavirus period when unemployment increased to 11%. There is increasing evidence that much of the cause of unemployment is due to a mismatch between skills demanded and the skills supplied. Contrary to popular opinion, manufacturing output has not decreased, rather, because of an increase in technology, such as the use of robots, and more efficient processes, fewer workers have been required to maintain or increase the level of output. The American labor force needs to be retrained. For example, instead of training people in mechanical skills, training should focus on computer skills and operating systems and controls. All of which is to say that, in the past, improved skills in the labor force contributed substantially to increased productivity. Currently, increased productivity is the result of increased use of capital and technology.

What is the importance of human capital?

Human capital is the collective knowledge, experience, skills, and behavioral attributes of the population. A significant contributor to human capital is the country's educational system.

There are three comments to be made about the United States educational system. During most of the 20th century, the K through 12 public school system proved to be superior and helped educate and train an excellent labor force. During the past forty years, the public school system, with many exceptions, has been in decline. Another way to express this issue is that students graduating from public schools are less prepared to make positive contributions to the economy. The third comment may seem contradictory. The college and university systems remain among the world's best. However, only 20% of high school graduates go on to attend and graduate from four-year colleges. The economy is as dependent on the 80% who do not go to college as it is on the 20% who do. Proving this 80% with the skills required is vital to maintaining a competitive economy and is another factor that will reduce the skill mismatch referred to above.

What about those folks who lack access to education facilities?

Will the poor always be with us? The permanent underclass of the population is estimated at 10% or 30 million people. Whether it be attributed to a lack of education, family upbringing, poor nutrition or lack of access to public health facilities or substance abuse, people who are mired in poverty frequently have no means of escaping their plight. To the extent that these circumstances persist, individuals will suffer, fail to meet their potential, It has become increasingly apparent that much of the structure of society, the culture and practices of both the public and private sectors present barriers to those seeking upward economic and social mobility.

Is the United States still a country of immigrants?

The United States, as we know it today, was built on the backs of immigrants primarily from Europe, Africa, and Asia. Yet, throughout our history, we have a record of closing the gates to newcomers. The debate today about the number of immigrants has serious economic impacts. There are sectors of the economy, which have traditionally been dependent on immigrant labor. Two that come to mind are agriculture, construction, and hospitality These labor-intensive industries have attracted seasonal workers who would come and go as the demand required. What with serious economic difficulties and challenging political instability in many Latin American countries, many of these immigrants have come and chosen to stay. The question arises, do these people displace traditional American workers or do they meet an unsatisfied demand for labor? Do these immigrants become dependents of the state? Do they use public services without contributing tax or payroll deductions? Alternatively, do they move in, assimilate and become responsible, contributing citizens?

At another level, corporations, universities, and hospitals are full of engineers, scientists, doctors and nurses who come from foreign shores. Not only do these immigrants make positive contributions, but they also raise the level of productivity in many significant ways.

What role does technological change have on productivity?

Technological change has three stages: Invention. Innovation, and Disbursement. Invention is the act of creating something new. It may be a product, a service or a process. Innovation is the act of enhancing, modifying or adapting an invention to a particular use. Disbursement is spreading or distributing the product or process into the marketplace.

Essentials of Macroeconomics

In many respects, changes in technology prior to WWII might best be described as mechanical and changes since WWII as technological. This over-simplification fails to incorporate conceptual changes in creativity that have occurred over the centuries, but it does serve to highlight the fact that changes in technology have multiplied exponentially since the invention of the computer. Prior to the industrial revolution, changes in technology were practically non-existent. At the beginning of this chapter we discussed the impact of the industrial revolution on economic development. Since the 1970s, almost two-thirds of increases in productivity have been attributed to the invention, innovation and disbursement of computer-based technology. Be it in communication, transportation, manufacturing, distribution, science or medicine, computer technology has produced more new products and processes than in all of the development of humankind over all of prior history.

Is our transportation system efficient?

An efficient transportation system is essential to the optimal delivery of raw materials, semi-finished products and final products to consumers as well as to moving people. Parts of the global system are highly efficient. Container ships transport goods in an efficient and cost-effective manner as heretofore unimagined. Super-tankers transport oil and railroads transport goods cheaply and efficiently. Airplanes are increasingly cost effective and move millions of people and cargo safely every day.

However, In the United States, the highway system is nearly broken. An unintended consequence of the interstate highway system was the urbanization of America. People moved from the inner cities to the suburbs. The effect of this population shift was to increase dependency on cars and trucks, to increase the wear and tear on roads, to increase pollution, and to increase American dependency on oil. Without serious improvements in infrastructure and decreased dependency on fuel guzzling transportation equipment, the United States runs the risk of becoming competitively disadvantaged relative to other economies.

Is healthcare an important factor with respect to growth and productivity?

Critical to an efficiently performing economy is the health and well-being of its population. Our healthcare system is made up of providers, such as nurses and physicians, hospitals, and clinics, and by insurers who protect people from bearing the full cost of medical treatment, costly procedures and medications. Both the public and private sectors are engaged as providers and insurers. Relative to other industrialized countries, the United States healthcare system is the most expensive in the world. The cost of healthcare is increasing at a faster rate than the rate of inflation. We have fewer doctors per capita than many other developed nations. Until the recently enacted healthcare measures, we had 40 million people uncovered for medical insurance. There is no measure in place that will reign in the costs of healthcare. The implications of this state of being will be of great importance to future wage earners and retirees. The increasing healthcare costs diminish our capacity to improve productivity.

How has the United States economy changed over time?

Until the industrial revolution, marked by the perfection of the steam engine in 1765, the US was an agrarian economy. For the next 100 years, the economy was essentially industrial, producing massive quantities of goods. Increasingly, during the post WWII era, the development of services, education, finance, insurance, health care, and real estate became major economic activities utilizing resources of land, labor and capital. Soon thereafter, particularly during the 1980s, the US became an information economy. Those with access to highly sophisticated computers amassed and processed huge quantities of data to contribute to decision-making, simulate scientific experiments and analyze causes and effects of multiple applications.

There are many who argue that an economy that is not highly productive in goods is a doomed economy. An economy that reduces its production of goods becomes more dependent on other economies to satisfy the demand for goods. Services are outputs that are intangible and have no shelf life. Services, which include healthcare, legal, accounting, education, social work, repair services, etc., are all labor intensive. If the performance of the service can be digitized, that is converted to electronic format such as in the case of accounting or legal research; the service can be outsourced easily to foreign countries. The question arises, how vulnerable is an economy if it increasingly relies on products and services of foreign origin? Part of the answer to that question is the degree to which increasing productivity in either the manufacturing sector or the service sector makes an economy more competitive and more self-sustaining.

What additional factors have an effect on the U.S. rate of growth?

Some factors to be considered as of 2020 are:

- The U.S. spends more on defense than the sum total of the next five highest defense-spending countries in the world.

- The U.S. consumes 25% of world oil production.

- The national debt of the U.S is greater than its GDP.

- Global warming and/or climate change threaten agricultural production, huge land masses vulnerable to rising seas, and shifting temperatures causing violent storms and fires.

- The emerging economies of Brazil, China, and India present new opportunities for trade and increased demand on global resources.

- The US population is aging with the ratio of workers to retirees decreasing.

- Income distribution is shifting so that the highest 10% of the population has a significantly disproportionate share of personal income and wealth.

Summary

Conventional wisdom dictates that an economy must grow to satisfy human wants, to provide for an improved quality of life and to be competitive in today's world. Productivity, the measure of output divided by input is the engine that drives economic growth. An economy can expand by bringing into use more resources, land, labor and capital, or it can expand with technological improvements. Through effective education and training, the United States has achieved increases in productivity beginning with the period after the Civil War but is waning now. Mechanical inventions such as the steam engine, the car, aircrafts, electricity and the telephone have enabled great advances in productivity. Although developed prior to WWII, it was not until the 1970s that the computer began to make immense contributions to productivity, the quality of life, and, indeed, to human behavior. The ability of the U.S. economy to remain competitive will largely depend on our continued invention, innovation, and disbursement of technological products and processes.

Moral dilemmas

1. Does economic growth uniformly affect all segments of the population?

2. What impacts do measures applied to achieve economic growth have on various segments of the population?

3. What economic measures should be applied to assimilate immigrants?

Moral Commentary

1. *Creative destruction* is a concept first articulated by economist Joseph Schumpeter. It describes a process whereby invention and innovation make previous goods or processes obsolete. The invention of the car

displaced producers of horse-drawn buggies and whips. Computers rendered the typewriter obsolete. Today, it is the cell phone that has made land-line phones obsolete. The consequences of this process are to render a wide range of resources, land, labor, and capital no longer in demand. Readdressing the question, does the worker serve the economy or is the function of the economy to serve the worker (?), How might those laborers displaced by creative destruction be protected or re-employed? Or, is it the fundamental principle of capitalism, that the market determines what is produced and how, without regard to the impact on any and all resources?

2. In many parts of the world traditional systems of distributing goods and services prevail; retail markets are composed of multiple specialists, small in size dispersed throughout communities. Likewise, services are provided by individual or small groups of professionals. In the United States retail markets are composed of giant firms such as Walmart and Target. Professional services, particularly in the health industry, are concentrated in large hospitals or health management organizations. The pursuit of higher productivity has implications far beyond the economy, such as the culture of a society and how its members relate and communicate. Is the drive for increased productivity always in the best interest of a society?

Chapter 10: Fiscal Policy and the National Debt

What is fiscal policy?

Fiscal policy is the management of the United States budget or flow of income and expenses. If income exceeds expenses then a budget surplus results. If income and expenses are equal then a balanced budget results. If expenses exceed income then a budget deficit results. Each year the Executive Branch of government sends a proposed annual budget to the Congress for its review and approval. In the budget are projections of income to be generated by taxes and other sources of revenue. Expenses projected by the federal government to deliver all services are itemized. Chapter five explained in some detail the sources of revenue and major expenses incurred by the federal government.

Since WWII, the fiscal policy of the United States government has been one of maintaining price stability, full employment and economic growth. As federal programs have increased and the role of the United States in maintaining global military security has expanded, the ability of the United States government to meet its primary objectives has become more complex. Over the past ten years the continued excess of expenditures over revenues has created ever-increasing deficits. These deficits are funded by borrowing from the Social Security Trust Fund and from private and public sectors in the United States and foreign countries. The national debt, which is the accumulated annual deficits, has increased to a level approximating 105% of GDP. The following discussion addresses fiscal policy and the national debt as if there were no constraints and that the federal government had considerable flexibility in applying fiscal policy.

Essentials of Macroeconomics

Under Keynesian theory, how should fiscal policy be implemented?

According to Keynesian theory, as mentioned in chapter two, during periods of economic expansion, the federal government should increase taxes and reduce expenditures. This action would give the federal government the capacity to respond during periods of recession by reducing taxes and increasing spending. Between 1946 and 2000, by and large, this is exactly the policy applied by the federal government. With varying degrees of success, in response to the recessions of 1948/49, 1963/54, 1957/58, 1960/61, 1969/70, and subsequently throughout the 1970s, 1980s, and 1990s the government reduced taxes and increased expenditures. Conversely, during intervening periods, the government increased taxes and either maintained or slightly reduced government spending.

What is the difference between a recessionary gap and an inflationary gap?

A gap is the measure of the difference between real economic output and the full potential of the economy. The full potential is the level of GDP if all available resources, land, labor and capital are utilized to their optimum capacity.

A recessionary gap is a negative difference when real output, which is the sum of $C + I + G + Xn$, is less than optimal potential GDP. During periods of recession, consumption decreases and firms produce and invest less. Total GDP is less than its optimal potential.

Exports, which are also a private sector factor, constitute only 14% of GDP. If foreign countries maintain or increase their demand for United States' goods and services, this may contribute to economic stability, but because the percentage of total GDP is small, the ability to mitigate or even reverse a recession by increasing exports is very limited. Consequently, the government must take initiatives to provide relief and reverse the recessionary trend.

Recessionary Gap

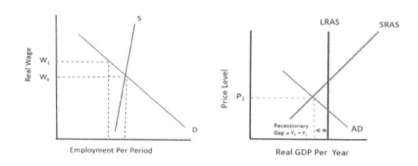

If employment is below the natural level, as shown in Panel (a), then output must be below its potential (S is supply, D is demand, We is less than W1). Panel (b) shows the recessionary gap $Y_P - Y_1$, which occurs when the aggregate demand curve AD and the short-run aggregate supply curve SRAS intersect to the left of the long-run aggregate supply curve LRAS.

An inflationary gap is the difference between real output and optimal potential GDP when output actually exceeds that optimal potential GDP. It is referred to as an inflationary gap because the level of output is unsustainable and will likely lead to rising prices as consumers' demand exceeds output and firms bid for scarce resources at higher and higher prices.

Inflationary Gap

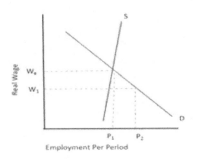
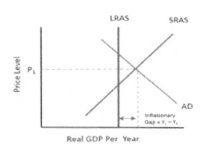

Panel (a) shows that if employment is above the natural level, then wages must be below optimum. The inflationary gap, shown in Panel (b), equals $Y_1 - Y_P$. The aggregate demand curve AD and the short-run aggregate supply curve SRAS intersect to the right of the long-run aggregate supply curve LRAS.

The question arises: does it take one dollar of tax reduction or one dollar of additional expenditure to increase GDP by one dollar? Or, conversely, will one dollar of tax increases or one dollar of reduced expenditures decrease GDP by one dollar? The answer is no! To understand this, it is necessary to begin with the concept of the average propensity to consume.

What is the average propensity to consume (APC)?

In previous chapters we have discussed: (1) Aggregate Demand. (2) Marginal Propensity to Consume, and (3) Equilibrium GDP. First, let us relate the marginal propensity to consume and aggregate demand. If you recall, after deducting taxes and social security from gross income, wage earners are left with disposable income. There are two choices wage earners face, to consume or to save.

The Average Propensity to Consume is another means of determining aggregate demand. In other words, aggregate demand is the amount of money individuals and families spend from their disposable income. What they do not spend they save. If disposable personal income equals 1.00, then the sum of consumption and savings must equal 1.00. The average propensity to consume in 2020 is about .96 and the average propensity to save, therefore, is .04.

When an individual spends one dollar, it does not stop there. For example, an individual has $100 on which he/she spends $50 for rent, $35 for food, and $11 for clothing. $4 goes into savings. The person receiving the rent money now has $50 to spend. He/she spends $25 on rent, $17.50 on food, $5.50 on clothing and saves $2.00. To solidify the example, the person receiving the rent money spends $12.50 on rent, $8.75 on food, $2.75 on clothing and saves $1.00. Carrying the numbers to their logical conclusion, the original $100 will generate a total of $2,500. Where did that number come from? In this example each individual is spending 96% of his/her income.

What are the marginal propensity to consume (MPC) and the multiplier effect?

The question arises, how do individuals behave when they receive an additional dollar of income? Do their consumption and savings patterns remain the same or do they change? The measurement of a change in consumption, given an additional dollar, is called the marginal propensity to consume. As one might infer, the measurement of a change in saving, given an additional dollar, is called the marginal propensity to save. Once again, the sum of the marginal propensity to consume and the marginal propensity to save is 1.00.

As an example, if an individual receives one additional dollar of income and chooses to spend $0.50 and save $0.50, then the Marginal Propensity to Consume would be .5 and the Marginal Propensity to Save would be .5. This leads us to define the multiplier effect. A change in income, increase or decrease, has a rippling effect throughout the economy. That is to say, that a change of $0.50, as cited above, passes on from the original consumer to others, buying and selling goods and services in the economy.

The formula for measuring the multiplier is:

$$Multiplier = 1/1\text{-}MPC$$

Let us put this concept to work in a practical application. If the GDP were at the $20 trillion level prior to a recession, and the impact of the recession were to create a recessionary gap of $500 billion (GDP = $19.5 trillion), how much would the government have to reduce taxes or increase spending to fill the gap; $500 billion or less? If the multiplier were to be 2, (Multiplier = 1/ (1-.5)) then the amount of tax cuts or increased spending need only be $250 billion ($500 billion/2).

Conversely, should there be an inflationary gap of $500 billion (optimum GDP is $20 billion, actual GDP is $20.5 billion), by how much would the government have to reduce spending? Multiplier =1/1-.5 = 2; therefore, $250 billion.

Do managing recessionary gaps and inflationary gaps always require initiatives by the Executive Branch and Congress each time the cycle shifts? No! There are certain built-in factors called automatic stabilizers.

What are automatic stabilizers?

Automatic stabilizers are adjustments to income which occur without requiring specific action by the government or the taxpayer. For example, income taxes are calculated on a marginal income basis. If one's income increases then the rate of taxation on the additional amount of income also increases. If one's income decreases, the marginal rate also decreases thus reducing the impact of the loss in income. Likewise, payroll taxes, which are applied as a percentage of income, will decline as income decreases. Once again, the impact of the loss in income will be reduced.

Corporate profits are taxed at a flat rate of 21% with a complex set of exclusions, waivers, and tax credits. In the event of a decrease in corporate income, the applicable taxes will also decrease.

Unemployment compensation is made available to provide financial relief to workers suffering from a loss of job. While it does not fully cover the lost income, it does provide relief and some degree of purchasing power for limited periods. Other types of transfer payments such as welfare, Medicaid and food stamps also kick in automatically.

Why is the marginal propensity to save important?

Especially during periods of economic expansion and, hopefully, an accompanying increase in personal income, individuals and families ought to increase the portion of disposable income saved. That is, their marginal propensity to save should increase and marginal propensity to consume decrease. A strong reason for setting aside money for savings is that of protecting oneself and one's family in the event of unforeseeable circumstances such as injury, medical expenses or loss of employment. Having a savings account to fall back on during a recession can provide important relief.

Credit availability may be another stabilizing factor. This suggestion presents two problems: One, it is very likely that a lender will withdraw credit availability in the event of loss of income or employment. Two, occurring additional debt during a period of unemployment, when the possibility of repayment is unknown, is a very unwise course of action.

What is discretionary fiscal policy?

The federal budget is divided into two parts: Entitlements and Discretionary.

Among other programs, entitlements include Social Security, Medicare, Medicaid, Welfare and Pharmaceutical Drug reimbursement. These programs are referred to as entitlements because their annual funding is mandated each year, unless the Executive Branch and the Congress agree to a program modification by legislative action. In 2020, entitlements accounted for 60% of the annual federal budget.

While it is not an entitlement, military expenditures constitute another 20% of the federal budget. Both the Executive Branch and the Congress are extremely reluctant to decrease military budgets. Consequently, that leaves only 20% of the annual federal budget to be treated as discretionary; that is, the portion that may be modified from year-to-year. In terms of real numbers, with a total budget of $4 trillion, $2.4 trillion is made up of entitlement programs; $800 billion is designated to the military, leaving another $800 billion as discretionary spending.

The $800 billion is allocated to cover expenses of the Executive Branch, Congress, and the Judicial Branch. In addition, most departments and administrative agencies are also included. While there is much discussion about government efficiency, or lack thereof, the amount of money in play is hardly adequate to implement fiscal policy effectively.

Changes in tax rates are another means of implementing fiscal policy. The progressive structure of income taxes has been an accepted and traditional form of income redistribution. The concept is one of taxing higher income recipients more than lower income earners to reflect different capacities to pay taxes. At one time in our history, during the 1960s, the marginal tax rate reached levels exceeding 80%. The highest marginal tax today is about 38%. Taxes have been increased during periods of economic prosperity, and taxes have been reduced during recessionary periods, such as during the late 1960s and the early 1980s, respectively.

Fiscal policy is the joint responsibility of both the Executive Branch and Congress. Because the Executive Branch presents a budget proposal to the Congress each year, one might interpret that opportunity as the first step in recommending fiscal policy. Thereafter, it is a negotiated process. As we get into discussions about the fiscal deficit, economic crises, and national debt, the ability to influence price stability, full employment, and economic growth will become clearer.

What are fiscal policy lags?

Lags are defined as the period of time that lapses before policy changes take effect. Lags can be relatively short, such as six to nine months, or relatively long, such as twelve months to two years. As a general rule, for example, tax credits, that is paying a taxpayer an amount of money in the form of tax relief has the most immediate effect. The IRS sends a check or electronically credits a taxpayer's account and the money in hand is spent, applied to a debt, or placed in a savings account. The next measure to have a relatively short lag is a reduction in the tax rate. This has a short-term lag because the amount of income tax deductions may change immediately. Increases in government spending have the longest lag period because of the time it takes to plan and execute new government programs.

What makes the lag periods important is the difficulty in measuring the outcome. As pointed out in chapter 15, the beginning of a business cycle is only recognized after the fact. Whether the cycle has peaked and entered a recession or bottomed out in the trough to enter a period of recovery, the timing of the specific event is not known when it occurs. Likewise, the duration of the cycle is also an unknown factor. Fiscal policy measures initiated to slow growth or to increase economic activity may be too little or too great, and rarely are just right.

Was the stimulus package of 2009 a form of fiscal policy?

Well after the fact, the recession of 2008 was determined to have begun in December 2007 and ended in June 2009, 18 months. Economists will argue forever about the causes and effects of the recession on both the United States and world economies. It is fair to say that after a long period of increased consumption, stagnant real wages, reliance on the increase of personal debt and a huge bubble in the housing market, housing and financial markets crumbled, creating a serious threat to the United States and world economies. A threatened collapse of major financial institutions coincided with the implosion of two out of three auto-makers and a more than doubling of the unemployment rate to 10%.

The government reacted by creating a $787 billion stimulus package consisting of $500 billion of increased spending and $287 billion in tax cuts. Based on our discussion of the multiplier and of lag periods, the total impact should have been about $1.6 trillion with a lag period of between 6 months and two years. But, wait a minute. The stimulus package was introduced in late 2009 and the recession was determined to have ended in June 2009. Did the package influence the economy? Perhaps the influence was psychological. In reality, the recovery from the recession was very sluggish and unemployment remained high at 9.5%. If anything, the stimulus package prevented the economy from entering a new recessionary period or from remaining even more lackluster.

The consequence of these programs was to increase the budget deficit by $1.4 trillion. In the ten years between 2001 and 2011, the national debt increased from $10.2 trillion to $14.5 trillion, or 42%. The national debt is now equal to 105% of GDP. Is this a cause of concern? What impact does the national debt have on future federal budgets and fiscal policy?

Do changes in fiscal policy always achieve their intended objectives, or what are some unintended consequences of changes in fiscal policy?

During recessions, decreases in taxes and increases in federal government spending are designed to increase disposable income and output, which should in turn increase employment. However, if individuals choose to save rather than spend, or to repay debt, rather than spend, the objective is thwarted. If increased spending results in greater use of capital or technology, then the goal is also thwarted.

During periods of economic expansion, increases in taxes may disproportionately affect various regions and sectors of the economy. Likewise, decreases in spending may have different impacts throughout the economy.

Was fiscal policy the only tool applied to reverse the recession of 2007?

What has been left out of the discussion was the $800 billion injected into the markets by the Federal Reserve Bank. This action was taken to restore stability in financial markets and to preserve the financial integrity of major financial institutions. Some institutions, such as Bear Stearns, were allowed to fail. Other institutions, such as Merrill Lynch, Loeb Rhodes, and Country Wide Mortgage were sold in distress sales to keep them afloat.

What is the deficit dilemma?

To begin with, there is no definitive maximum amount of an annual budget deficit or the national debt. That is to say, there is no formula, no law, and no third-party agency that determines what number or when a deficit or debt becomes excessive. The factors that create a dilemma are the same market factors as supply and demand. On the one hand citizens require and/or depend on a certain level of government services. On the other hand are the concerns of taxpayers and creditors who generate the funds to pay for those services.

Essentials of Macroeconomics

For thirty-five years, between 1945 and 1980, the government alternately generated surpluses and incurred deficits. The United States enjoyed a prolonged period of economic growth and the real income of the average American family increased. A period of high inflation and extremely high interest rates, 22 to 24% at the end of the 1970s and early 1980s, led to a period of financial austerity. This was followed by huge annual budget deficits, which persisted at a declining rate until 1998 when, once again, surpluses were generated for two successive years. Instead of being applied to reduce the national debt, the surplus was placed in a reserve to be spent in subsequent years.

Deficits are funded by increasing the national debt. Debt instruments, which are obligations of the United States Treasury, are issued with maturities varying between one month and 30 years. The United States dollar is also a debt instrument, and as fiat currency, it has no maturity. Unless there is a budget surplus, maturing obligations plus the interest due are rolled over into new Treasury Obligations. The funding of this debt is dependent on the trust and confidence of investors that markets for the debt will always be liquid and those investors may sell their debt at any time and at prices that may produce profits or losses, but in any event are close to 100% of cost. The dilemma about the deficit is one of testing the limits of investors' willingness to purchase Treasury Obligations at a reasonable market rate of return.

What is modern monetary theory?

Recently, there has re-emerged the notion or argument that the size of annual federal deficits and resulting increase in the national debt are inconsequential. The argument goes on to expound that repayment of the national debt is a matter of no concern; that the primary concern of the federal government is to achieve full employment. In this pursuit, the federal government should be unhindered in printing currency and borrowing funds. Once full employment is achieved, to avoid inflation, the government can increase taxes, and raise interest rates.

Many economists take issue with the theory, arguing that increased debt either causes an increase in the general market level of interest rates, an increase in inflation, or generates an increase in the cost of debt service due to higher interest returns required by holders of Treasury obligations. The fact that United States debt is denominated in United States dollars should not be a justification for lack of the federal government managing the budget. in a responsible manner.

Who invests in the national debt?

One can go online and view The United States National Debt Clock" which displays the increase in debt minute-by-minute. In August 2020 it was $26.2 trillion. The largest holder of Treasury obligations is the Social Security Trust Fund and other United States government agencies. The second largest holders are Americans. The third largest holder is the Federal Reserve Bank. Among the largest international holders are the Chinese Government with about $1.4 trillion, followed by the Japanese with about $0.7 trillion. In recent years, the largest investors have been foreign governments.

Three factors to be kept in mind regarding the national debt: One, the debt is denominated in United States dollars. Two, the debt has been considered by investors to be the highest rated debt or a debt without default risk. Three, in a worst-case scenario, the debt can be reduced by increasing taxes or printing money, neither of which is a particularly desirable solution.

What is the effect on financial markets if the government increases or decreases the national debt?

The final economic discussion of this chapter is one addressing the effects of borrowing and retiring Treasury obligations on financial markets. Creating new obligations or increasing the national debt is referred to as having a crowding-out effect on markets. Retiring or repaying the Treasury obligations is referred to as having a crowding-in effect. In reality, financial capital markets have been able to absorb simultaneous increases in raising funds; that is without any crowding-out effect.

To understand this phenomenon, one has to visualize a global financial market fixed in size and supply of investment dollars. Entering into this market are entities from two sectors: the private sector and the public sector. If the supply of dollars is fixed and the demand for dollars increases by borrowing of the Treasury, the effect will be that of causing interest rates to increase. This crowding-out of the private sector by the public sector causes an increase in the borrowing costs to the private sector. In the reverse scenario, should the Treasury retire or repay debt it will be increasing the supply of dollars in the market, which will have the effect of decreasing interest rates. This crowding-in effect decreases the cost of borrowing for the private sector.

Summary

Fiscal policy, budget deficits and the national debt are all part of one picture. Unless there is a will to increase tax revenue or decrease spending, the sustainability of government services will depend on government borrowing. This in turn will require continued investor confidence. The limits of investor confidence are communicated through the financial markets by the level of interest investors require to satisfy their tolerance for risk. This discussion has tried to avoid the political differences that have an overbearing influence over economic issues regarding price stability, full employment and sustainable economic growth.

Moral Dilemmas

1.   Do recessionary gaps affect regions and sectors of the economy universally and evenly, or are there disparities?

2.   Do the concepts of marginal propensity to consume and to save apply to all levels of income, or are some levels more able to change propensities than others?

3.   Are there some demographic groups that are more intensive recipients of entitlement programs than others? Are there alternative means of satisfying these groups' needs?

4.   Do federal government initiatives to stimulate the economy have equal and universal effects throughout the economy, or are there disparities? Should the federal government take initiatives to address these disparities?

Moral Commentary

1.   The great recession of 2007 – 2009 was largely attributed to a housing bubble. For simplicity's sake, let's leave it at that. A substantial amount of the mortgages underwritten were funded by collateralized mortgage obligations (CMO). When those CMOs began to fail, the entire market froze. The loss of liquidity threatened the banking system, as banks had heavily invested in the long-term bond obligations. The cause of the failure was the inability of borrowers to repay their debt and as a result, many of them lost their homes. Part of the solution to the bank liquidity threat was for the Federal Reserve Bank to purchase the CMOs to the tune of $800 billion. The purchase money went to the lenders. Very little of the money was used to provide relief to the home-owners. What measures might the government have initiated to address the borrowers' financial distress rather than that of the lenders?

2.   As pointed out in the chapter, 60% of the federal budget is composed of entitlement programs. The first entitlement program, introduced in 1935, was social security. It addressed the needs of the disabled and those over the age of 65 in the midst of the depression. Since WWII, many programs have been added to address needs such as childcare, nutrition, health care, income security and

veteran benefits. To what extent should the government provide these services? Should the programs expand or contract? Who and how should the programs be funded?

Chapter 11: Money and Banking

"One rule which woe betides the banker who fails to heed it.
Never lend money to anybody, unless he doesn't need it."
-Ogden Nash

Is money the root of all evil?

Maybe not, but it surely ranks right up there with other causes of evil. What is money? Is it real or virtual? How did money come into being? Who creates money? What is the role of money in our economy? What is the money supply? What are the functions of financial institutions? All of these questions will be addressed in this chapter.

What is money?

Money is a medium of exchange. Instead of trading goods and services for one another, money is used to purchase and sell those goods and services. Money is a standard of value. Prices of goods and services are quoted in dollars. Wages are paid in dollars, as are all contracts in the United States. Money is a store of value. Because money is a medium of exchange and standard of value, individuals, firms and public entities are willing to hold money for indefinite periods of time, relying on the fact that the purchasing power of money will not significantly decline over that period. The bottom line is that the value of money is measured by society's trust in the government that issues it. Money is referred to as fiat money because a government arbitrarily determines what the currency shall be and declares it to be so. The government is thereafter responsible for preserving the value of that currency.

The argument over the use of money versus the barter system is pretty simple. If you can imagine the butcher, the baker and the candlestick maker each trading in each other's goods, how would the prices be determined? Clearly, the seller would have one price in mind and the buyer would have another. Each transaction would have to be individually negotiated and, certainly, the exchanges between the three parties would each have different values attached to them. Enter the use of money. Now there is a standard medium of exchange whereby the price, as measured in money, is universally the same.

Is money real or virtual?

In reality, money is both. Real money, as we know it, is the tangible coins and currency we possess. The intangible or virtual money is that contained in our bank accounts, and the transactions we execute with credit and debit cards.

What is the money supply?

Money is not just coins and currency. When we pay bills, such as for credit cards, utilities, or rent, we rarely use cash. Most of us either write checks or make electronic payments against deposit balances held in banks or credit unions. About half of the money supply is coin and currency and the other half is bank deposits.

How is the supply of money measured?

The money supply is measured in three categories:

1. M1 is composed of coins and currency, checking account balances, and negotiable orders of withdrawal accounts (NOW). You might call this cash or near cash.

2. M2 includes M1 plus savings accounts, time deposits of less than $100,000 and money market mutual funds held by individuals. Time deposits differ from savings accounts because they are specific contracts between the bank and the depositor with respect to amount, maturity and interest rate. Now we have cash, near cash, and accounts that can readily be converted to cash.

3. M3 includes M2 and time deposits in amounts greater than $100,000. Because time deposits are contracts fixed in time or maturity, amounts, and rates of interest, they are not as easily converted to cash. Usually, there is a penalty for early termination of a time deposit, especially those that exceed $100,000 in amount.

It is important for the money supply to be balanced with the size of the economy (GDP). Too little money would impede transactions, cause prices to fall and interest rates to rise. Too much money would cause prices to rise and interest rates to decline. Much like any other commodity, the value of money is determined by the balance between supply and demand.

What is the demand for money?

There are three types of demand for money: One is the transactional demand. This form of demand results from the daily needs of individuals, firms and public entities to execute purchases and sales of goods and services. Two is the precautionary demand. This demand emanates from a need to save or accumulate money for future use. Three is the speculative demand. Because the value of money changes in large or small degrees relative to money or currencies of other nations, there are individuals and firms that trade in multiple currencies much like individuals trade in other commodities. Profits or losses are incurred based on one's expectation of the future value of money.

In this context there are four factors that influence the demand for money:

1. Inflation, which is, as you may recall, an increase in the general level of prices. It is also a measure of the decrease in purchasing power of money.

2. Income, which is the total amount of disposable income of an individual, influences the amount of money one needs to satisfy one's living requirements. Generally, the higher the level of income, the more money one demands.

3. The interest rate will influence the demand for money. At low interest rates individuals and firms are more inclined to borrow money. At higher interest rates, the demand for money decreases. Conversely, at low interest rates people are disinclined to save, which inclination changes as interest rates increase.

4. Credit availability is not only a function of interest rates, but also a function of lenders' willingness to undertake risk. If the supply of money is high and the demand for money is low, interest rates will be low making lenders reluctant to lend for medium and long terms. With an increase in demand and the accompanying higher interest rates, lenders should be more willing to increase credit availability.

What is the circular flow of money?

Money, in the form of income earned, rent received, dividends and interest earned or goods and services produced and sold is either spent or saved. The portion that is spent is exchanged for goods and services. Picture two concentric wheels, one moving clockwise and the other counter-clockwise. If both wheels are not moving, that is, if consumers stop spending money, or firms stop producing goods and services, the economy comes to a roaring halt. At its optimal level, the amount of money and the velocity with which it changes hands must be in balance with the prices and quantity of goods and services supplied and demanded.

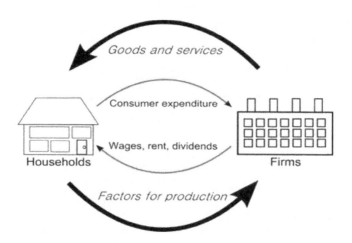

What are the functions of financial institutions?

First a little history: Banking begins and ends with the word "trust." When trade of goods and services first converted from barter to the use of precious metals such as gold and silver, carrying these heavy metals over great distances was cumbersome. Consequently, traders looked for trustworthy individuals with whom they would store their gold and precious metals. These goldsmiths, for a price, would store gold in their vaults. Two events arose out of these transactions. First of all, the goldsmiths would issue receipts confirming the gold deposits. These receipts gained negotiable value so that instead of actually delivering gold for payment, the receipts would be exchanged while the gold remained on deposit. Secondly, the goldsmiths came to realize that the gold would sit on deposit for longer periods of time and not all receipts were redeemed at the same time. This afforded an opportunity to lend the gold to third parties, always with the expectation that repayment would occur prior to having to deliver the gold to the original depositor. The goldsmiths were, in fact, creating money.

Essentials of Macroeconomics

Without going into great detail, from that beginning private banking houses developed and the role of bankers in facilitating trade evolved throughout the world. Leap forward to modern times in the United States and we encounter a financial industry composed not only of banks, but also mutual funds, hedge funds, pension funds, insurance companies and brokerage houses that provide banking services in one form or another. For purposes of this discussion, we shall concentrate on the functions of banks.

What distinguishes banks from other financial institutions?

Banks take three different forms: Commercial banks, which are regulated either by the Comptroller of the Currency, The Federal Reserve, or the Federal Deposit Insurance Corporation (FDIC); Savings Banks, which are regulated by the Comptroller of the Currency and the FDIC; and Credit Unions, which are regulated by the National Credit Union Association.

There are more than 4,700 commercial banks in the U.S. The largest ten of those banks hold more than 50% of the total deposits in the system and more than 60% of the total assets. Two other classes of banks are part of the banking system: Mutual Savings Banks, which were created to provide depository and lending services to common people, and which specialize in mortgage lending, and Credit Unions, which were formed to provide banking services to employees of corporations and to members of communities.

The other institutions mentioned above, mutual funds, pension funds, insurance companies, and brokerage houses provide different financial services and abide by different regulators and regulations.

What is the primary function of banks?

The primary function of banks has traditionally been that of a financial intermediary. Banks take in deposits from customers with an abundance of cash and lend those funds to customers in need of cash. The depositors look exclusively to the bank to retrieve their money and the borrowers are beholden to the banks to repay their debts. The banker profits by paying low rates of interest to depositors and charging higher rates to borrowers. Since the 1970s, banks have expanded the variety of services they perform to include foreign currency trading, purchase and sale of securities, cash management, and credit card services, to name a few.

What is bank regulation, and why are banks regulated?

After the stock market crash of 1929, and during the first years of the Great Depression, over 3,000 banks failed. The question facing the federal government was one of how to restore public confidence in banks and in the banking system. A safe and sound banking system was considered to be critical to a vibrant and sustainable economy. At the time there were both state and nationally chartered banks. Interstate banking did not exist. In fact, a relatively small portion of the population held bank accounts. Most bank depositors were either upper income or wealthy individuals or business entities.

The first measure to restore confidence was the creation of the Federal Deposit Insurance Corporation (FDIC). Initially, deposit accounts were insured for up to $10,000 ($180,000 in today's value) which, at the time, was an adequate amount. Today, the FDIC insures deposits for up to $250,000. The insurance protects individuals from losses in the event a bank fails. On this basis, an individual can be completely indifferent about the bank where he or she deposits money. The banks themselves pay for the insurance through an assessment applied by the FDIC.

Having insured depositors against losses, what should the FDIC do to protect itself against loss?

The answer to this question is one of regulating and supervising banks and bankers. For all practical purposes, banks are not authorized to accept deposits without having FDIC insurance. The FDIC promulgates regulations governing the acceptance of deposits and the use of funds for investment or lending purposes. It requires banks to hold reserves against potential loan or investment losses, and it requires banks to have a minimum level of capital in relation to its liabilities and total assets. Banks are inspected periodically and either given a satisfactory rating or required to make changes and adjustments to meet FDIC requirements.

Over the years, with the expansion of the U.S. economy, the development of multinational enterprises and increase in global trade, and advances in technology, the banks and the banking system have changed radically. Interstate and international banking are now pervasive. Electronic payments, either through on-line banking or automatic teller machines (ATMs) are commonplace. Banks and corporations move billions of dollars and other currencies from one institution to another daily. New regulations and new regulatory procedures frequently lag the introduction of new technologies. From time-to-time banks fail and their assets and liabilities are absorbed by another bank without any interruption in service.

How effective have bank regulations been?

Since WWII, there have been two national disasters with respect to the banking system. The first occurred in the late 1980s and early 1990s. Savings and Loans institutions (S&Ls) were created back in the 1920s to accept deposits and create mortgage loans. The purpose was to help the American family acquire home ownership. Until 1980 the interest rates that banks and S&Ls could pay on deposits were regulated. Ceilings were established to set the highest interest rates banks could pay. In 1980 the regulation governing interest rates was eliminated. S&Ls, which held long-term mortgage loans at low fixed rates of interest funded by low interest rates on savings accounts, were faced with having to pay higher interest rates to attract and maintain deposits. To make up for this pending disaster, that is, mortgage loans earning less than the costs of funds supporting them, the S&Ls entered the commercial loan arena and began making a large number of loans at very high rates of interest to cover the negative spread on their mortgage loans. Amazingly enough, it took ten years for the results of this folly to come home to roost. Many borrowers defaulted and hundreds of S&Ls were closed. The FDIC created a new corporation to assume the assets of the closed S&Ls and to liquidate them in an orderly fashion. The total cost of the liquidation exceeded $45 billion.

The second national disaster commenced in August 2007. In 1983, two investment banking organizations created a debt instrument called a Collateralized Mortgage Obligation (CMO). This debt instrument was secured by multiple mortgage loans extended to individuals and families and carried no guaranty of the issuer. Its purpose was to expand the source of funding mortgages beyond the deposits held by traditional mortgage lenders; that is, banks, savings and loans entities and credit unions. Because a CMO was secured by so many individual mortgages, and because historically mortgage loans had a very low default experience, the CMOs were sold at low coupons, or market rates of interest. Many of the underlying mortgages were extended to people in amounts they could not afford, or to purchase houses at greatly inflated prices. It was virtually inevitable that borrowers would not be able to repay their loans.

After the first of the CMOs failed, it did not take long for the entire market of CMOs to cascade to the point where no institution was willing to purchase the instruments. Investment portfolios of banks, which held substantial amounts of the CMOs, became illiquid. Faced with the quandary of a potential systemic collapse, the Federal Reserve Bank guaranteed the portfolios and became the banker of last resort to restore liquidity. Bank failures were averted and confidence restored.

Subsequently, a general collapse of the mortgage market ensued. The federal government injected more than $800 billion dollars into the banking system to maintain stability. A number of institutions were closed, placed in receivership, or sold to larger banking corporations. New regulations were promulgated in Congress in the form of the Franks-Dodd Bill which was designed to foresee and prevent future systemic threats. The applications of the many features of the bill continue to be reexamined with a great deal of dispute about the degree of regulation and limitations on banking practices.

Summary

Money, be it in the form of coin, currency, or bank deposits is essential to the efficient performance of a market economy. Payments, whether made manually at a store counter, by check, credit card, debit card or in electronic form have evolved to accommodate an ever-growing domestic and global economy. Banks, which had their initial formation in the hands of goldsmiths, have evolved to multi-trillion-dollar institutions with offices across the country and the world. Massive bank failures have threatened the United States economy and, consequently, given rise to the need for regulation and supervision. In the United States, deposit insurance has been the vehicle of maintaining public trust and confidence in banks and the banking system. Developments in modern technology have presented new challenges to regulators in maintaining a vigil over bank assets, liabilities and operations. The imposition of new rules and regulations is an ongoing process.

Moral Dilemmas

1.   Important market, social and ethical issues arise when examining the practices and policies of banks, raising the question: Are banking services equally affordable and accessible to all segments of the population?

2.   With such concentration of market power in the largest ten institutions, do markets behave efficiently and equitably?

3.   Do depositors maximize their interest rates? Do borrowers obtain the lowest rates possible in a freely competitive market?

4.   Is money loaned equitably among large, medium and small borrowers?

5.   Are the standards and practices uniform among all classes of depositors and borrowers?

Moral Commentary

1.   Banking services generally are not available to people of lower income. Branches are not located in poorer communities. Banks do not facilitate federal electronic transfers through low or zero balance accounts for social security, welfare or veteran benefit programs. Banks do not provide pay-day loans or facilitate immigrant transfers to families back home. Should all of these services be universally accessible and affordable?

2.   With so much concentration of power, percent of deposits and of assets, in the ten largest banks, what is the effect on competition with respect to rates of interest paid and interest rates on consumer loans and credit cards? Do banks, abiding by the Community Reinvestment Act, an act requiring banks to reinvest funds (deposits) back into the community from which they are received. proactively extend credit to and in minority communities?

Chapter 12: The Fed, Monetary Policy, and Financial Regulation

Countries all over the world have central banks to manage their money supply, provide services to private and public banks, in some cases provide regulatory oversight, and to manage monetary policy. In the case of the United States, the central bank is called the Federal Reserve Bank (the Fed).

What is the Federal Reserve System?

After suffering many years of economic crises and monetary instability, in 1913 the United States Congress passed the Federal Reserve Act which created a system of twelve district banks. If you can picture a country that was still very regional in focus; That was undergoing the transition of communication via telegraph to telephone; That had no interstate highway system: In which horse and buggy were still competing with cars and trucks; and although the airplane was invented in 1903, there was no commercial air service; then you have a reasonable understanding of the lack of geographic and economic integration of the United States in 1913. Under these conditions, to serve the county effectively, it was necessary to establish regional or district offices of the Fed.

The districts were designated by geographic proximity, population density, and economic activity. Eight of the districts were east of the Mississippi River. Boston,

MA; New York, NY; Philadelphia, PA; Washington, D.C.; St Louis, MO; and Chicago, IL. Each of the districts represented commercial, financial, governmental and agricultural interests. Richmond, VA and Atlanta, GA served the South. The four districts west of the Mississippi were: Minneapolis, MN; Kansas City, MO; Dallas, TX; and San Francisco, CA.

The structure of the Federal Reserve System is unique to the United States. Each of the District Banks is owned by member banks which come from the private sector. The member banks elect a board of directors which chooses the officers. The entire system, however, is overseen by a Board of Governors, who are appointed by the United States President, confirmed by the United States Senate, and serve for a period of fourteen years. By having staggered terms of fourteen years, each governor serves beyond terms of elected officials (Congressional Representatives - 2 years, Senators – 6 years, and the President – 4 years). Once appointed and confirmed, the governors are no longer beholden to any elected official. In effect, the Fed, as an autonomous creation of the United States government, acts virtually as a fourth arm of government: Congress, Executive, Judicial and the Fed.

What are the functions of the Federal Reserve System?
The Fed has five functions:

1. Establish and implement monetary policy.
2. Serve as the lender of last resort, historically to the banking sector only.
3. Issue currency. This used to be, but no longer is a function of the Treasury Department.
4. Provide banking services, principally payment clearing, to the banking sector.
5. Supervise and regulate the financial sector.

Essentials of Macroeconomics

How does the Fed establish and implement monetary policy?

The Fed has three tools with which to implement monetary policy:

One is the establishment of a legal reserve requirement. All banks must maintain a certain amount of cash, either in their vaults or with the Fed. The reserve requirements have two impacts on banks. The first is that of providing cash, liquidity, to meet the withdrawal demands of depositors. The second is to limit the amount of funds available for investing or lending. By changing the reserve requirements, the Fed is able to influence the amount of money banks are able to create. This particular tool is used rarely because there is a long lag period between initiating a change and its real effect in the economy.

Two is the use of the discount rate, which is the rate of interest charged to banks that borrow funds from the Fed. In point of fact, few banks borrow from the Fed. For very short-term purposes, there is a huge market in Federal Funds, which are funds loaned and borrowed (sold and purchased) overnight among banks. Banks, which have a surplus of cash, lend to those which have a temporary shortage at very low interest rates. Resorting to use of the Fed discount window is considered a sign of weakness in the banking sector. Consequently, banks avoid use of the Fed. For this reason, while the discount rate may be modified from time to time, it serves as an indicator of Fed policy, more than as a tool of significant effect.

Three, the most frequently used tool, is that of purchasing and selling United States Treasury obligations in the open market. We shall discuss use of this tool more expansively in a later chapter. For the time being, a quick and dirty explanation is that the purchase of United States Treasury obligations is a means by which the Fed injects money into the banking system. The sale of United States Treasury obligations is a means of extracting money from the banking system or reducing the money supply. Use of this tool has an immediate psychological and material impact on financial markets.

Essentials of Macroeconomics

How is money created and destroyed?

Fundamental to the ability of the banking system to create money is the fact that not all depositors withdraw their money at once or at the same time. If you recall the discussion about the goldsmiths in chapter 11, once they discovered that receipts they issued were being used as currency, and that the gold placed on deposit with them stayed for extended periods of time and was not withdrawn in great quantities at one time, the goldsmiths started lending the gold entrusted to them to third parties. The present-day banking system works on the same principle.

As an example, let us say that the Fed has established a reserve requirement of 10%. A customer makes a deposit of $10,000. The banker, bank A, places $1,000 in reserves and lends out $9,000. The borrower places the $9,000 on deposit in another bank, bank B. Bank B places $900 in reserve and lends $8,100 to another borrower, who, in turn deposits the funds with bank C. Bank C places $810 in reserves and lends $7,290, and so forth, until, at the conclusion of the process, the initial $10,000 has multiplied to$100,000. In this form, the banking system has literally created $90,000 in new money.

The destruction of money is the reverse of the above. If the Fed were to increase the reserve requirement from 10% to 20%, the amount of money banks could lend would be reduced. In fact, banks would only be able to increase the money supply to $50,000. The process of reducing banks' capacity to lend is called money destruction.

This deposit expansion or money creation is called the Deposit Expansion Multiplier. The formula for calculating the multiplier is:

Money Expansion Multiplier = 1/reserve requirement (ratio)

Essentials of Macroeconomics

This process is called fractional reserve banking. Once again, it is based on the principle that not all depositors withdraw their money at the same time.

I mentioned that the Fed does not change or modify reserve requirements frequently because of the long lag period required to take effect. An additional reason for not changing reserve requirements is because banks, out of their own prudence, maintain significant portions of their assets in the form of liquid investments. Typically, these investments amount to 15% to 20% of total assets. Those investments are mostly in United States Treasury obligations with maturities ranging from one month to thirty years. There is a huge market, in the trillions of dollars, for buying and selling these securities, at fair market prices, on a daily basis. Banks requiring additional cash can sell securities at a moment's notice and convert the securities to cash. It is because of this fact that the most frequently used tool for implementing monetary policy is the purchase and sale of United States Treasury obligations on the open market, not modifying reserve requirements.

What are open-market operations?

Establishing and implementing monetary policy is one of the most critical responsibilities of the Fed. Monetary policy is the vehicle by which the Fed influences interest rates for the purpose of reducing the risk of high inflation and optimizing economic growth. During periods of rapid economic growth, the Fed may choose to slow down the rate of growth by trying to push interest rates higher. During periods of economic contraction or recession, it is likely that the Fed will try to lower interest rates. Remember that higher rates of interest encourage savings while discouraging borrowing, and that lower interest rates are a disincentive to savers while encouraging borrowing. The "Goldilocks rate" is that rate at which individuals are motivated to save and individuals and firms are willing to borrow.

There are two interest rates on which the Fed, through its Federal Open-Market Committee (FOMC), focuses. One rate is the discount rate, which the Fed determines arbitrarily. The second is the Fed Funds rate, which the Fed can only target or influence. Since the Fed Funds rate is determined by supply and demand factors in a freely traded market, the Fed can only establish a target rate, and initiate action to achieve that rate. Because of its overwhelming financial power, the Fed usually achieves its goals.

How do Fed operations implement FOMC monetary policy objectives?

Among the assets held by the Fed are trillions of dollars of Treasury obligations and bonds or debt instruments issued by the private sector. Minimally eight times a year, or on an as-needed basis, the Federal Open Market Committee (FOMC) meets to evaluate the economy and to determine whether or not to change interest rates. If the economy appears to be contracting, that is, if GDP is decreasing, then the Fed will elect to lower interest rates by increasing the money supply, that is, purchasing Treasury obligations. As in any freely competitive market, the increase in supply of a good will cause its price to decline. The Fed enters the market and purchases Treasury obligations with cash. Banks and corporations, which sell Treasuries to the Fed, will receive cash. The immediate, short-term effect is to increase the supply of cash reserves banks hold with the Fed, which in turn, will contribute to an increase in Fed funds among banks. The Fed Funds rate will fall and, accordingly, banks will lower their prime lending rate to corporate customers in an attempt to increase loanable assets and thereby increase interest income.

What is the prime lending rate?

Step aside for a moment. Banks have a wide array of customers ranging from very large, financially strong corporations to firms and individuals of lower credit quality. Those corporations of the very highest financial strength negotiate the very lowest rates of interest from their bankers. Indeed, these corporations work with a number of banks and will direct their business to those institutions offering the most preferential interest rates. In order to avoid a bidding war, banks tacitly agree on the lowest rate at which they are willing to lend. This rate is referred to as the prime rate and is quoted daily in many business publications. In a freely competitive market, firms are prohibited from colluding. It is important to understand that a tacit agreement, such as that of the banks to apply the prime rate, is an economically sensible solution to avoid price wars that might contribute to instability.

Because there is a greater supply of money, interest rates will decline and borrowing should increase. I say "should," because there is no law of the marketplace that says firms must borrow just because rates are lower. The process of causing interest rates to decline has no assurance that it will achieve economic growth. Certainly, the decision not to lower interest rates will impede economic growth by discouraging investors from borrowing and expanding productive capacity.

Should the economy become overheated; that is, should economic growth become too accelerated, creating uncertainty and a fear of inflation, the Fed may determine to decrease the money supply and attempt to drive interest rates higher. In this event, the Fed sells Treasury obligations in the financial markets. Firms and individuals who purchase the obligations reduce their cash holdings.

Do the Federal Reserve Banks pay interest on cash reserves on deposit?
Historically, the Fed has not paid interest on reserve deposits. During the recession of 2008 and on into 2009 and 2010, banks were awash with excess funds. While it was in the interest of economic growth to see the banks lend some of this money to credit worthy clients, there was also a concern that if too much money were loaned at once there might ensue a high level of inflation. To induce the banks to keep some of their excess funds on reserve, the Fed commenced paying interest on those deposits. The initial rates were low, at 0.25%. However,

as the Fed funds rate changed, the Fed also modified its interest rate on reserve deposits.

How effective has the Fed been in fighting inflation and recession?

A modest level of inflation, that is, an inflation rate of 3 – 5% has been considered tolerable. Indeed, some economists argue that a modest level of inflation is healthy for the economy. Since WWII there have been three periods of double-digit inflation. Inflation reached 18% in 1948, 12% in 1974, and almost 15% in 1980. The Fed Funds rates reached 9.13% in 1974 and 20% in 1980 (data for 1948 is unavailable). The prime rate was 2% in 1948, 12% in 1974, and 20.3% in 1980. In all three episodes the inflation rates, fed funds rates and prime rates were reduced to modest levels within short periods of time, usually about one year to 19 months. The most painful post-WWII period of inflation was between 1979 and 1981. The actions of the FOMC were certainly critical to taming inflation and returning the economy to stability. Since fiscal policy also influences economic behavior, to attribute the restoration of stability entirely to monetary policy is probably an exaggeration.

What is the historical importance of the Depository Institutions Deregulation and Monetary Control Act of 1980 and the Banking Act of 1999?

To quote an oft abused phrase, the Depository Institutions Deregulation and Monetary Control Act of 1980 "leveled the playing field." The act unified regulations and practices of heretofore distinctly different institutions. Commercial banks, Savings and Loan Institutions, and Savings Banks, the latter two frequently referred to as thrifts, had separate and distinct charters and functions. As competition among them increased, it became apparent that the different regulations gave some a competitive advantage. Although there were three key provisions, a fourth led to severe unintended consequences.

- All depository institutions became subject to Federal Reserve requirements.
- All depository institutions were authorized to issue checking accounts.
- All depository institutions enjoyed equal access to all Fed membership privileges.

The fourth action was to remove restrictions on interest rates paid by the thrifts. The consequence of this action, as discussed in chapter 11, was to place thrifts in the untenable position of competing for deposits at high rates of interest while being saddled with large portfolios of fixed low rate mortgage loans to fund. It took ten years for the disastrous results to play out, but eventually many thrifts failed. The old adage of 3 – 6 – 3, pay 3% interest on deposits, charge 6% interest on loans, and be out on the golf course by 3 in the afternoon, was broken.

In its wisdom, in 1999 the Congress passed the Banking Act of 1999. This act extended Fed jurisdiction to insurance companies, pension funds, investment companies, securities brokers and finance companies. Much of this new legislation made a great deal of sense. Over the years since 1945 the market share of deposits and management of money had diminished among banks and diversified to other financial institutions. Consequently, it became increasingly difficult for the Fed to implement monetary policy operating exclusively through the banking sector. Another portion of the Act also contributed to unintended or unforeseen consequences. That was the repeal of the Glass-Steagall Act of 1933, under which investment banking functions could not be performed by commercial banks. The thinking was that large bank holding companies had the capacity to separate these two functions under the same roof and that the market would be better served by allowing commercial banks to compete with investment banks, securities firms, insurance companies, and brokerage houses. There is much contention among regulators, elected officials and economists about the impact of this Act on markets and the general economy.

What are Monetary Policy lags?

As discussed earlier, the use of different monetary policy tools produces results over different periods of time. Part of the reason for the lags is the time it takes to implement the policy change and for that change to work its way through the system. A change in the reserve requirement may increase or decrease the system's capacity to lend and create or destroy money. However, to the extent that banks have self-imposed liquidity requirements which exceed reserve requirements, this measure has limited effectiveness. Frequently, modifications in the reserve requirement have taken six to twelve months to achieve the desired results.

Since many institutions, and more particularly the larger ones who command the greater market share, do not use the discount window, changing the discount rate, while having an immediate effect, also has limited impact. Changes in the discount rate have a short lag time of as little as one month.

Thus, it is the monetary policy implemented by the FOMC that focuses on money supply as it influences market interest rates that has the most immediate and measurable effect. Often, the market anticipates FOMC actions in the form of repricing Fed funds rates. As the Fed funds rates change, there is an almost immediate change in prime lending rates. However, changes in the lending patterns, affecting all classes of commercial and consumer loans, may take many months to occur.

How do Monetary Policy and Fiscal Policy interrelate?

Both monetary policy and fiscal policy strive to achieve full employment, minimal inflation and optimal economic growth. By relying on changes in taxing and spending policies, the federal government is seeking to increase or decrease the amount of disposable income to consumers who, as you should recall, make up 70% of GDP expenditures. The lag time of changes in fiscal policies can endure one to three years before being fully effective. In addition, the results are more difficult to measure.

Monetary policy addresses banking and corporate activities by stimulating borrowing and investment or by de-stimulating these activities. The former is designed to induce economic expansion and ultimately job creation by lowering interest rates. The latter has the opposite effect, which is that of purposely slowing down economic growth to create a more stable economic environment.

What were the housing bubble, subprime mortgage and subsequent financial crises of 2008 all about?
Books are being written to explain the convergence of these three events.

The housing bubble can best be described as a chase for bigger and fancier homes by people who were reaching beyond their financial means to realize the "American Dream." Demand exceeded supply leading to ever-increasing home prices. Just as is the case of a balloon, once pressure exceeds the balloon's capacity, it bursts. The resulting crash led to massive foreclosures, people being forced out of their homes, and an inventory of unsold real estate that took years to be absorbed.

The subprime mortgage crisis relates to the housing bubble insofar as the credit instruments created to provide loans to the home purchasers were bundled into Collateralized Mortgage Obligations (CMOs), which were sold to many unwitting investors as obligations with a representation of a very low probability of default. As each individual mortgage backing or guaranteeing the CMO defaulted, the CMO itself became uncollectible. The resulting unforeseen inability to service (repay) the debt led to a total market collapse.

Essentials of Macroeconomics

The financial crisis is the third leg of the stool. Banks and governments around the world had loaded their balance sheets with the above described CMOs. In addition, a new form of investment vehicle, the Credit Default Swap (CDS), a kind of insurance against loan losses, had become a defensive strategy to reduce loan exposure. With the collapse of the housing market and the market for CMOs, a number of investment firms faced imminent failure. Those who issued CDS instruments were unable to meet their obligations. Heretofore liquid, marketable assets held by banks lost value because there were no buyers. Global financial markets were threatened with massive failure, beginning with the United States financial system.

My spin attributes the financial debacle of the years 2007 through 2009 to three factors:

1. A sixty-year cycle of ever-increasing use of debt by American consumers to attain a quality of life, which eventually exceeded their ability to sustain.
2. The combination of financial entities and consumer driven firms enabled this process by offering increasingly generous amounts of credit at ever decreasing lending standards.
3. The decline of internal standards and controls compounded by the absence of regulatory oversight over a wide-range of financial entities and instruments.

How was normal functioning restored to financial markets?

The U.S Congress authorized the Treasury Department to initiate dramatic action in the form of the Troubled Assets Relief Program (TARP). The CMOs and other similar instruments, characterized as "toxic" because there was no market to buy and or sell the instruments, were purchased by the Treasury to the tune of $700 billion. The purpose was to restore liquidity to the banking system and to avert a more serious recession. This is only part of the story.

What should be done about the housing market?

With one out of every eleven homes in foreclosure and with the housing market being one of the largest single markets attracting consumer dollars, restoring stability to this market was a priority objective. There were three programs aimed at this priority:

1. Assisting four million families who were at risk of losing their homes.
2. Helping homeowners who owed more than the market value of their homes.
3. Bailing out Sallie Mae and Freddie Mac, two government sponsored mortgage investors, which provided the major funding source to primary mortgage lenders.

These programs worked to the extent of minimizing institutional failure and restoring faith and functionality to the financial system. Where the programs fell short was in restoring financial solvency to many abandoned homeowners. There was much frustration among the various participants in the mortgage market from homeowners to loan service organizations, to lenders, and to investors because solutions were perceived as preferential, irresolute and inadequate.

Was this an opportunity for significant financial sector and regulatory reform?

If ever an opportunity to "strike while the iron is hot," the year 2010 was it. Some progress was made in the passage of the Dodd-Frank Bill. It provided for:

- A Consumer Finance Protection Bureau (CFPB) with strong, independent oversight for consumer, mortgage, credit cards, and payday loans.
- Power to break up firms that might create financial chaos.
- A Financial Services Oversight Council to provide warnings in the event potential trouble was anticipated.

- Restriction to 3% of the amount banks may invest in hedge and other private equity funds
- Termination of weak or loose lending practices
- Requirement that firms creating CMOs or other types of collateralized debt obligations retain at least a 5% vested interest in such instruments. Colloquially, this is called "skin in the game."

The actual implementation of the Dodd-Frank is still in process, ten years later. Consequently, the efficacy of the legislation is yet to be determined.

What is the dual banking system?

A discussion of the banking system is incomplete without addressing what is referred to as the dual banking system. Banks may be organized under national banking regulations or state banking regulations. Historically, states chartered banks dating back to the formation of the country. National banks were viewed by some as potentially contributing to too much concentration of financial power. National banks finally gained recognition in 1863. Thus began a form of competition with bank organizers seeking the most advantageous regulations among various states and the National Bank Act. Today, while state-chartered banks look to the state as the primary regulator, in fact the requirement of FDIC insurance for all depository institutions significantly reduces any differences in regulatory enforcement among state and nationally chartered entities.

Summary

Monetary policy as enacted by the Federal Reserve Board of Governors and implemented through the Federal Reserve System is a vital ingredient to maintaining a stable and sustainable economy. The independence of the members of the Board of Governors was seen as critical to avoiding political influence over decisions rendered by the governors.

However, as witnessed in the recent past, all of the regulations and all of the efforts expended by regulators have not been sufficient to avoid periodic bouts of inflation, nor threats of financial systemic collapse. The questions to be addressed by students are those of how free of regulation should markets be to provide equal opportunity for all competitors and to what extent is the economy at risk when regulations are inadequate or regulators choose to ignore those regulations.

Moral Dilemmas

1.   Do the tools available to the Fed to implement monetary policy have uniform impact on all sectors and the economy, or are there disparate impacts?

2.   What is the effect of a tightening monetary policy on existing debt; that is, if interest rates rise, how do individuals and firms manage the increase cost of debt service?

3.   If the Fed ignored inflationary trends and inflation increased unabated, who would suffer the most, and who might be able to weather the storm?

4.   When access to credit is readily available, both in amounts and low interest rates, should institutions or individuals and firms be primarily responsible for pilling on excess debt?

5.   In the crisis of 2008, should the government and the Fed have been more focused on helping the borrowers rather than the lenders?

Moral Commentary

1.   Since 2002, the Fed has, from time-to-time, maintained a policy of low interest rates as a means of stimulating economic growth. With nominal rates hovering around one percent, real rates have actually been negative; Nominal rate of 1% less CPI of 1.5% equals negative 0.5%. Not only do these rates reduce the

value of accumulated savings but they also act as a stimulation to spend rather than save. Furthermore, the measures penalize people who are living off of lifetime savings or dependent on fixed incomes. Is this a fair trade-off? Should or should there not be a provision to accommodate those suffering from these unintended consequences?

2.   During periods when for whatever reasons the Congress has refused or been unwilling to increase spending to stimulate the economy, the Fed has stepped into the breach. Without getting into the political ramifications, in the absence of Congressional action, does the Fed have either an economic or moral obligation to act?

3.   The CFPB regulates a host of financial institutions: Banks, credit unions, payday lenders, mortgage servicing operations, and debt collectors. The benchmark for falling under CFPB compliance regulations is $10 billion. Since its enactment in 2011, CFPB has processed more than 730,000 complaints, and issued $7.7 billion in enforcement actions. Many of the nation's largest and most prominent financial entities have been fined: Bank of America, JPMorgan Chase, Wells Fargo Bank, to name a few. Management of financial institutions argue that CFPB is both arbitrary, and unnecessary. Are banks and other financial institutions indeed able to regulate themselves? Do consumers need advocates for their complaints and concerns? Are fines a sufficient mechanism to cause those regulated to conform to CFPB policies and "mend their ways"?

Chapter 13: International Trade

One of the least recognized innovations of the 20th century was the shipping container. An ordinary box, the size of a truck trailer, placed in the hold or on the deck of a steam ship, radically accelerated world trade. A steam ship that took one week to unload and another week to reload with manual labor now takes two days. Fragile products can be shipped more safely, theft is reduced, and containers can travel from manufacturing sites to a foreign distribution center without packing, unpacking and repacking.

The importance of international trade and how it is accomplished is the subject of this chapter. The world is a better place to live for several reasons: One, trading partners become so interdependent that they rarely declare war against each other. Two, trade allows for nations and economies to specialize in what they do best and purchase from others what otherwise would be very costly to produce. Three, consumers can acquire goods and services more cheaply. Four, in selling to foreign markets producers employ more resources, including labor.

Not all nations' borders are open to free trade. For a variety of reasons, many nations erect protective barriers to prevent or reduce the volume of foreign products permitted to enter. Conversely, in the interest of reciprocity and economic growth, many nations have eliminated or significantly reduced barriers to trade.

Essentials of Macroeconomics

What is the history of international trade in the United States?

International trade is the buying and selling, the importing and exporting, of goods and services among foreign countries. For example, our neighbor to the north, Canada, is our largest trading partner. Since the settling of the country, the United States has engaged in trade. Initially, we produced cotton, shipped it to England where it was processed into textiles, which in turn were exported to the United States as finished goods. During our formative years, it was typical for the United States to export raw materials, principally agricultural products, and to import finished products.

Fast forward to more recent times. In the 20th century, the United States became a net exporter and primary source of credit to the world. After WWI we increased exports of military goods, and manufactured goods to include transportation vehicles. Especially after WWII, when most of the productive capacity of Western Europe and Asia had been destroyed, the United States became the world supplier of heavy and light equipment, steel, processed aluminum and many other basic materials necessary to rebuild economies. For twenty years after WWII the United States was a self-reliant producer of oil. Until 1975 the United States had a favorable balance of trade.

What is the balance of trade?

The balance of trade is the net difference between the total value of goods and services sold to other countries (exports) and the total value of goods and services purchased from other countries (imports). On a global basis, the net balance of trade is zero. While it may be desirable for all countries to have a favorable balance of trade, that is, a surplus, in a practical sense, that is not feasible.

How is the balance of trade measured?

- Exports exceed imports = Surplus or a favorable balance of trade
- Exports equal imports = An even balance of trade

Essentials of Macroeconomics

- Imports exceed exports = Deficit or an unfavorable balance of trade

The United States balance of trade shifted from favorable to unfavorable in 1975 for four reasons:

1. The restored economies of Western Europe and Asia were competing with United States producers globally.

2. The growth of the United States economy surpassed its ability to provide sufficient oil to meet the demand.

3. With the formation of Oil Producing Export Countries (OPEC), an international cartel, oil production was decreased and, in the space of one year, prices of oil tripled.

4. United States. consumers developed insatiable appetites for foreign goods.

The unfavorable balance of trade has persisted consistently since 1975. In fact, it increased from modest levels of negative $100 billion to ever increasing amounts of $800 billion per annum. Only during the recession of 2007 to 2009 did the amount decrease to about $400 billion. We have mentioned imports as being the primary culprit exacerbating the negative trade balance. Relative to other nations, United States exports are large in absolute terms. Recently, United States exports have amounted to $1.8 trillion. As a percentage of GDP, however, they amount to only 14%. We have allowed other countries to swallow our market share and, as will be covered more extensively in microeconomics, multinational corporations have moved much of their production offshore, thus diminishing further exports of U.S. produced goods and services.

What has been the United States government policy with respect to trade?

Over time the United States government trade policy has shifted from periodic emphasis on protectionism to a more open borders trade policy. Trade policy can take essentially four forms:

1.   Managing imports with tariffs, quotas and bureaucratic standards.

2.   Stimulating exports through tax incentives, subsidies, and credit.

3.   Engaging in multilateral trade negotiations globally.

4.   Engaging in bi-lateral, nation-to-nation trade agreements

In 1974 the United States became a signatory to the General Agreement on Tariffs and Trade (GATT). From that date on trade barriers have been consistently reduced. GATT rules prohibit subsidizing the production of goods exclusively for export purposes. Through the United States Export Import Bank, modest amounts of credit have been granted to United States manufacturers.

What is the theory behind international trade?

As long as 240 years ago, Adam Smith theorized that nations should export what they have in abundance and import from other nations what they lack or to fill a scarcity. By so doing, nations can specialize and produce more for less. This theory addresses both the notions of absolute advantage and comparative advantage.

Absolute advantage has two characteristics: One form of absolute advantage is that of possessing natural resources such as coal, iron, copper, or bauxite. It also includes climate and the availability of water. The second form is that of being able to produce a product using fewer resources. In both cases, absolute advantage is not permanent, but transitory. At one time, the United States was self-sufficient in copper. After electrifying America, we depleted our copper resources and we are now dependent on Chile for the supply of copper. Another example is the effect of *La Niña* current along the Pacific coast of South America. This warm water current creates immense climate shifts ranging from extreme rainfall in some areas and draughts in others. The Humboldt Current is a cold water current flowing northerly along the west coast of South America. It affords an absolute advantage to Peru because anchovies populate the current. *La Niña* refers to a shift in the Humboldt Current westerly, creating a warmer climate pushing the anchovies further offshore. The absolute advantage is diminished.

Comparative advantage occurs when two or more countries produce different goods at the lowest opportunity cost. You may recall that in chapter eight we introduced the production possibilities curve. Using a simple example of producing two goods, the production possibilities curve demonstrates that, given a fixed amount of resources, more of one good cannot be produced without sacrificing the production of the other good. Thus, production can be increased to the point where more of the alternate good is sacrificed or given up than is gained by the increasing output of the primary good. Comparative advantage is an extension of that same argument. The GDP of a country will be maximized as long as the opportunity costs do not exceed those of another nation or economy.

Is there an argument in favor of or supporting protectionism?

There are several arguments supporting protectionism. Not all of them pertain to either the United States or all countries, in general.

- After the fall of the Berlin Wall in 1989, the United States became *de facto* the world's most powerful nation militarily, as well as economically. For national security purposes, it is argued that the United States should protect those industries that produce goods vital to its military preparation.

Modern technology and the manufacture of arms, munitions, electronic equipment, and aircrafts, for example, are among those industries. The logic is one of answering the question, "What would a country do if it were dependent on a foreign nation to supply any product critical to its national security"?

- Many developing nations suffer from a lack of resources, inadequate financial capital and small markets. These nations, in particular, argue that in order for infant industries to increase their production to satisfactory levels of economies of scale, those infant industries need protection. The theory is that, once those infant industries mature, protection will no longer be needed.

- Among the developed nations, the United States has a relatively high cost of living. To maintain a stable standard of living the American worker needs protection against goods and services produced in low wage countries. The argument is difficult to sustain on purely a wage basis. Products which are labor intensive can and are produced for less in countries in Asia, Africa and Latin America. Products which are capital intensive are produced in countries with similar wage levels to the United States The solution to the threat of lower wages is based on increased productivity either through higher level of skills, more intensive use of capital, or technology.

What are protectionist measures?

Protectionism is the act of limiting the imports of goods and services. It can take many forms. Six examples are:

1. Tariffs, which are a form of tax imposed on imported goods as a percentage of the value of those imports. Tariffs are product specific.

Revenue tariffs are designed to generate income and are imposed on products not competing with domestic production. A typical example is the tariff imposed on the alcoholic beverage scotch, which is a product of Scotland. Restrictive tariffs are designed to protect the United States' industries from cheaper produced foreign goods. The effect of the tariff is to raise the price to the consumer that is equal to or greater than the domestically produced goods.

2. Quotas are restrictions on the amount of a good that may be imported. If aggregate domestic supply is insufficient to meet aggregate domestic demand, there is a need to allow the importation of that good. An example of such a good is sugar. Domestic sugar production is not only insufficient to meet demand, it is also produced at a cost significantly higher than global costs. To protect and preserve domestic production, quotas on imported sugar are imposed to assure the sale of domestically produced sugar at a price exceeding the cost (profit margin).

3. Bureaucratic measures may be imposed to require that certain products meet national standards, or that products be inspected prior to permitting entry. These types of measures apply to pharmaceutical products as well as fruits and vegetables and other food products.

4. Voluntary restraints are self-imposed export restrictions to appease the importing country. In the 1970s, with a sudden and serious increase in the cost of gas, American demand for small, fuel efficient cars increased dramatically. Japanese producers were poised to capture this demand while United States producers were caught off-guard. To allow United States producers time to modify design and production, the Japanese were asked and acquiesced to a 10% restriction on the annual increase of car imports to the United States.

5. Trade embargoes and sanctions are politically driven policies designed to isolate a country from trading with the United States either with its exports to the United States or United States exports to that country. The most noteworthy example of this policy has been the United States embargo on Cuba, which has lasted almost sixty years.

6. Cultural or taste preferences have also played a role in restricting trade. Because of their size, United States cars have been unattractive in European markets. The Japanese take huge pride in home produced products, making it difficult for any foreign manufactures to penetrate the Japanese market.

In general, economists argue that free trade benefits all, while trade restrictions inhibit a country and an economy from reaching optimal GDP levels. Free trade forces domestic producers to seek the lowest costs of production. Free trade enables consumers to purchase goods and services at their lowest costs. Free trade allows a nation to specialize in what it does best given its resources. Global GDP is maximized through the process of free trade.

While these arguments sound persuasive, not all countries derive the same benefit from free trade. Generally, large countries benefit more than small countries. The open doors of a free trade policy cause pain on some in the short-run. Entire industries have been reduced or wiped out. In the case of the United States, our textile industry has been practically eliminated. We no longer produce consumer electronic equipment. Much of our tool and die industry has been decimated. On the other hand, we are major manufacturers of computer chips, commercial aircraft, chemicals and agricultural products. To the extent that we have a major share of the global market for these products, other countries are reliant on us and do not have a significant participation in those industries. Furthermore, it can be argued that as a consequence of being a major proponent of free trade, we have contributed to our own trade deficit.

What are the principal factors contributing to the United States trade imbalance?

As pointed out earlier, the United States entered a period of on-going trade deficits in 1975. Before discussing the various factors contributing to this situation, it is important to understand how the United States has been able to sustain this trend. The United States has been and continues to be the world's largest economy, although the Peoples' Republic of China is rapidly catching up. Our share of world GDP stands at 15% in 2020. Our share has been declining with the growth of European economies and those of the emerging countries such as China, India, and Brazil.

The United States continues to be a safe haven for foreign investors. If you recall the discussion of the circular flow of money in chapter eleven, you will understand how the United States manages its trade imbalance. The wheel moving counterclockwise is the revenue generated by the sale of exports and the investments of foreign governments, individuals and corporations in United States government securities and bond and equities markets. The wheel moving clockwise represents the purchase of foreign goods and services and funds investments in foreign markets. All of which is to say that we can continue our dependency on foreign goods and services until we no longer are able to borrow the money or sell exports in foreign markets to create revenue with which to pay for those imports. That is to say that there is a balance between income flows and goods and services purchased.

Given the above, the following are six causes of the current United States trade imbalance:

As pointed out in chapter three, consumption, at a 70% level, is the largest factor contributing to our GDP. Household income increased almost continuously from 1945, the end of WWII, to 1975 when it leveled off. Even then, with increased borrowing capacity, consumers continued to spend significant amounts. Along with the purchase of domestic products such as homes, appliances and cars, there was a huge demand for foreign products ranging from cars, to electronic equipment, textiles, and computers.

As the United states economy grew, our dependency on energy also increased. We have coal reserves to meet our needs for decades to come, but with the advent of fracking, we are able to reduce our reliance on coal and shift to alternative energy sources. However, our dependence on cars for land transportation, on oil byproducts such as chemicals and plastics, and on commercial airlines for air transportation caused the increase in the demand for oil to exceed domestic supply in an ever-increasing amount. Only during periods of recession has the demand for oil decreased. With the introduction of new technology, fracking, the United States has, once again, become a net exporter of oil and gas.

Our educational system is a dichotomy of bad and good. At the same time that our public education system at grade levels K through 12 is deteriorating, our university system, both public and private, continues to be the envy of the world. In the past, many foreigners who came to study in the U.S. remained and became strong contributors to our economy. The trend has reversed. Now, many foreigners come to study and then return home to contribute to those economies with which we compete.

Multinational companies are those corporate entities which have headquarters in one country and operate production facilities in foreign countries. In an overly simplistic explanation, it can be stated that there are two major reasons for expanding overseas: One reason is to take advantage of cheaper resources. For the most part, those resources are labor, but they might be raw materials, as well. The second reason is to manufacture products closer to the markets in which they are being sold. Regardless, the extent to which production is shifted overseas it contributes to our growing trade imbalance.

It may sound strange to say that the rate of economic growth in the United States has contributed to our trade imbalance. How? With increased productivity contributing to higher wages came increased consumption, that is, with increased purchasing power came an increase in the demand for imports.

There is widespread concern about the loss of a manufacturing base in the United States economy. In the 1970s, the big three, GM, Ford, and Chrysler had over 90% of the United States auto market. Today, that number is less than 50%. We no longer produce TVs, household electronics, toys, textiles, and the list goes on. With the loss of some industries came also the loss of jobs. While those jobs were gone, new opportunities arose, particularly in health care, financial services, and in small companies providing computer related software design and support services.

How does our trade deficit relate to Asia?

Beginning in 1975, Japan became the leader among Asian nations in making major inroads in the American market. The Japanese manufactured cheaper and increasingly higher quality cars and household electronic equipment. Their initiatives were followed by the Taiwanese, North Koreans, Chinese of Hong Kong, and other Asian nations. The Japanese themselves became so proficient in penetrating foreign markets that their manufacturing and managerial practices were emulated in many multinational companies.

In the early 1990's, a period of stagnant economic growth, and to some extent deflation, commenced in Japan. This event marked two significant shifts: The amount of Japanese exports to the United States leveled off and the Chinese invaded the United States' markets in an astonishing show of competitiveness in price, quality, and quantity. Because of a very close relationship with Japan following WWII, no doubt further enhanced by the lack of a Japanese military and dependency on the United States for national security, the United States and Japan have viewed one another as strong allies and trading partners. At the same time, the United States' relationship with the Chinese has been cast in the shadows of hope, expectation, opportunity, doubt and trepidation. Like Wal-Mart entering small communities and threatening the livelihood of mom and pop stores, China entered the United States market threatening entire industries.

As the world's most populated country with 1.3 billion inhabitants, and a per capita income of barely $5K, China not only has a large population of cheap labor, but also represents investment opportunities for economic growth in heretofore unforeseen proportions. By maintaining an artificially low rate of exchange with the United States dollars, China kept its products cheap to United States consumers for an extended period of time. The temptation to retaliate or apply protectionist measures to prevent this continued growth in Chinese exports has been undermined by the fact that the Chinese have purchased a significant portion of United States treasuries which finance that very trade deficit, and powerful United States corporations are determined to invest and participate in the economic growth and expansion of China.

The emergence of the People's Republic of China on the global scene presents a multitude of threats to the prevailing world order:

1. As the Chinese economy grows and a larger percentage of its population participates in that growth, the demand for a larger share of world resources is inevitable.

2. As a command economy, that is an economy in which the state through ownership has a prevailing interest, China is able to subsidize or

otherwise support industries to give them a market advantage not available in free market economies.

3. The state-controlled markets can dictate terms and conditions, limiting foreign investment and participation. Requiring firms to disclose private technology is one example.

4. From time to time currency manipulation has been a method applied to give Chinese produced goods a market advantage.

5. China has frequently been accused of theft of intellectual property, principally technology.

Summary

Since its founding, our nation has been built on our capacity to trade. At the same time, the large geographic expanse of the U.S. enabled the county to absorb population growth and build the world's largest economy based primarily on domestic production and consumption. As other parts of the world, primarily Europe, Asia, and parts of South America have successfully developed their own economies, the United States' share of global GDP has begun to shrink. During the last 35 years of this 250-year saga, a favorable balance of trade has reversed and now United States imports exceed exports. For a period of time, this imbalance did not seem to be a cause of alarm. The questions now arise: How long can such a trade imbalance be sustained? What can be done to reverse the trend? What is the threat to the overall United States economy? As in the case of other questions raised in this course, these questions go to the heart of the study of economics and the satisfaction of unlimited human wants given scarce resources.

Moral Dilemmas

1.   Why do the same individuals who have lost their jobs to foreign producers purchase foreign goods?

2.   In the search for less expensive resources, principally labor, is there a moral obligation to assist those who are displaced or whose skills have become uncompetitive?

3.   As in the case of sugar, should a quota system be applied, thus driving up the cost of the product to all consumers, or should a subsidy be granted to preserve the industry?

4.   With increased demand for the world's resources, how can the needs of emerging economies such as China, India, and Brazil be met while still satisfying United States requirements?

Moral Commentary

1.   Wages are not the only labor related costs that drive up the cost of production in the United States. Related to wages are the number of hours a laborer may work before receiving overtime compensation. Medical and retirement benefits also increase labor costs, as do safety and general working conditions. Low labor cost nations, such as those located in Southeast Asia, Africa, and Latin America, do not have minimum wage laws, child labor laws or other regulations governing working conditions. Should United States importers of goods from those countries impose on foreign producers' standards and practices similar to those in the United States?

2.   From time-to-time, the United States government, for political reasons, imposes sanctions on foreign countries. North Korea, Cuba, and Iran serve as good examples. In addition to affecting seriously the lives of citizens in those

countries, the sanctions put United States firms at competitive disadvantages with respect to access to resources and to foreign markets. Should or should not those firms be compensated for these losses?

3.   Container ships and mammoth oil tankers sail the seas safely and unimpeded because the United States Navy guards major shipping lanes throughout the globe. The costs of this protection are borne by the United States taxpayer. Should the United States government seek some compensation for providing this security to exporters and importers of nations all over the world?

Chapter 14: International Finance

International finance, as opposed to domestic finance, is the use of multiple currencies and multiple markets to satisfy the following demand:

- To fund the purchase and sale of goods and services traded among foreign countries.

- To fund direct foreign investments of multinational corporations that are establishing operating subsidiaries and affiliates in foreign countries.

- To fund investments made by foreign governments, central banks, corporations and individuals in bonds and equities issued and sold in various foreign markets.

- To provide financial intermediary services by accepting deposits and making funds available in the form of loans, both short-term and long-term, to borrowers in foreign countries.

- To permit speculators to enter and exit international financial markets and exploit perceived opportunities to make profits.

- To facilitate the transfer of funds, be they remittances back home, dividend and interest payments, or general transfers among individuals, firms, and governments.

Essentials of Macroeconomics

It is essential to understand that every country determines in what currency contracts may be denominated and payments settled. For example, in the United States our legal currency is the dollar. That means that all payments for the purchase and sale of goods and services, and all contracts may be satisfied and paid for in United States dollars, not foreign denominated currencies. In Great Britain the same rules apply to the pound, in Japan the yen, and in China the yuan or renminbi. Some countries share a common currency as is the case of 19 European nations which use the euro. Some countries have adopted the United States dollar, as is the case of Panama, Ecuador and El Salvador.

What this means is that a debt in Japan cannot be settled in dollars, nor can one in Great Britain be settled in dollars. An exception to the above is the fact that certain commodities, such as oil, sugar and coffee are bought and sold in United States dollars. As a dominant global currency, trading in one currency has added stability to the markets of those commodities.

Because of the increase in global trading and investments, it has become necessary to establish mechanisms and markets that can manage the flow of funds and provide stable and reliable markets to satisfy all participants.

What are the mechanics of international finance?

Foreign trade is the exchange of goods and services between two or more countries. Unlike national or domestic trade, goods and services that are bought and sold internationally have two cost factors. One factor is the cost of producing the goods or services in their country of origin. The second factor is the rate of exchange between the dollar, in the case of the United States, and the local currency. Generally speaking, there is no difficulty in exchanging dollars for euros, yen, British pounds, or Canadian dollars. Those currencies are bought and sold in the billions of dollars day in and day out. The rates of exchange may vary, but usually within a narrow range.

Essentials of Macroeconomics

Foreign trade transactions may be executed on a cash basis, usually with a bank transfer, or on a credit basis, whereby either the buyer or the seller obtains credit to purchase or to produce a good or service. Because there is a geographic distance and a time lag between purchase and delivery there arises the issue of executing payment and receiving goods. When the two parties have traded frequently and have developed a mutual trust, then the payment and delivery are no longer an issue. In the event that buyer and seller do not know each other there emerges the concern of what comes first, payment or delivery. This gap or lack of trust is bridged by using a bank as an intermediary. The buyer deposits payment with a bank and funds are not released until delivery is complete. This is a bit of an over-simplification, but it captures the essence of bridging the confidence or trust gap.

In executing a direct foreign investment, a multinational corporation transfers dollars from a bank account in the United States and instructs the banker to buy a foreign currency, let's say euros, to be credited to an account of that same corporation in Germany. The euros are then used to purchase a firm or to build a plant and equipment to manufacture goods in the local market.

In the event that the cost of borrowing euros, that is the rate of interest prevailing in the euro currency market, may be less than borrowing in dollars, the same multinational corporation alluded to above may approach a German bank and borrow euros to purchase the local firm or build a plant. Once the company is up and running, part of the income generated will be used to repay the loan.

Investors who wish to purchase shares of a foreign corporation follow a similar procedure. They instruct their United States banker to sell dollars and buy, let's say, Swedish krona to purchase shares of Electrolux in Sweden.

Because the rates of exchange among dollars, euros, pounds, and yen fluctuate daily, speculators perceive opportunities to make profits. If a speculator expects that the dollar is losing value against the pound, he/she might sell dollars for pounds, at an exchange rate determined today with a future delivery date when the cost of the dollars is less than in today's market. On or before the future date (settlement date) the speculator will sell the pounds and repurchase the dollars at a more favorable rate of exchange (if the speculator is right). The speculator has no interest in a trade transaction or any kind of investment. The speculator is strictly making a bet. He/she may make or lose money based on what the rate of exchange is on the day of settlement of the transaction. As you might imagine, if the speculator expects the dollar to increase in value over time, he/she will buy dollars at an exchange rate determined today for future delivery and thereby gain from that position.

What is the balance of payments?

In chapter 13 we discussed international trade and the balance of trade. The total sum of cash flows of a nation with all other nations is called the balance of payments. Relative to corporate accounting, you might look at the balance of payments as similar to a cash flow or a statement of source and use of funds. The balance of trade is referred to as the current account, and the remaining portion is referred to as a capital account.

Balance of Payments

Current account

Exports

Imports

Subtotal Balance of trade

Outgoing transfers

Payments to individuals

Dividend, interest payments

Government transfers

Incoming transfers

Payments to individuals

Dividend, interest payments

Government transfers

Total Current Account

Capital account

Long-term corporate transfers (net of sent and received)

Long-term government transfers (net of sent and received)

Capital transfers in the form of loans and investments (net)

Total balance of payments nets to zero

To understand the last statement, that the total balance of payments nets to zero, it is necessary to explain that any trade deficit is paid for by a capital account surplus. In effect, the United States borrows the funds used to pay for the excess of imports purchased over exports sold from foreign sources. Those countries which enjoy a balance of trade surplus, as in the case of China, are net exporters of capital account transfers. If you wish to take it a step further, the net balance of payments globally is also zero.

How are rates of exchange determined among nations and their currencies?

As the world has become a smaller place, and as trade and international investing have increased exponentially, exchanging currencies, particularly among strong or reserve currencies, has become increasingly simple and markets have become relatively stable. Conversely, it was not too long ago, fifty years and beyond, that exchanging currencies was relatively complicated and markets were very volatile.

Rates of exchange, which are the price or cost of buying one currency with another, are determined by the same law of supply and demand as applies to any markets of commodities or the buying and selling of goods and services. Even today, this application is not universal and, as the following discussion will describe, getting to the degree of efficiency of today's foreign exchange markets was not an easy task.

Are all currencies exchanged in a freely floating system?

Freely floating systems are similar to open and competitive markets. Without interference, usually from governmental authorities, currencies are bought and sold among banks, central banks, brokers, dealers, and private parties. Some governments intervene and prevent their currencies from being freely traded. These governments typically are those located in developing or emerging countries that suffer from serious balance of trade deficits as a consequence of lack of demand for their exports. Impoverished nations suffering from lack of resources fit into this category.

How did we evolve to the freely floating exchange system of today?

Modern technology permits instantaneous execution of foreign exchange transactions in many currencies and with many institutions all over the world. It has not always been that way. If one puts into perspective the history of the development of communication systems and the invention and dispersion of modern technology, one can more easily understand the evolutionary process.

As we have discussed, for a variety of reasons, nations chose to establish their own independent currencies, referred to as fiat money. Given this state of affairs, it was difficult to execute foreign trade transactions with currency values fluctuating wildly. In an attempt to mitigate this volatility, many nations agreed to put their currencies on a gold standard. Why gold? Because it was perceived to be a rare metal that preserved its market value. This meant that central banks would strive to maintain a constant price or value of their currencies relative to an ounce of gold. For example, the United States set a price of one ounce of gold being worth $32.00. Technically, if one was uncertain of the stability of the value of the dollar, one could submit $32 to the Federal Reserve Bank and demand one ounce of gold. Nations which maintained a fixed ratio between their currencies and their gold supply were adhering to a gold standard.

Maintaining a gold standard can be very arbitrary and difficult to manage. The benefits of the gold standard were those of facilitating international trade and maintaining monetary or currency stability at home. The drawbacks of the gold standard were:

- If exports exceeded imports then the exporting country's gold stock was increased, which could cause an inflationary increase in the money supply.

- If imports exceeded exports then the importing country's gold stock would decrease as it shipped gold to the exporting countries, thus decreasing the money supply and impairing economic growth.

- Likewise, if the gold stock did not increase relative to the growth of the economy then the economy itself would suffer.

- Adherence to the gold standard was blind to the business cycles and periods of inflation and unemployment experienced by its participants.

- Adherence to the gold standard negated any practical implementation of a monetary policy.

At the conclusion of WWII, the International Monetary Fund was created at Bretton Woods (New Hampshire). The purpose of the fund was to supervise an international exchange system by pegging currency rates of exchange to the United States dollar. The dollar would maintain a gold convertibility ratio of $35 to the ounce. Thus, indirectly, foreign currencies pegged to the dollar maintained convertibility to gold, as well. If foreign currencies gained value relative to the dollar, they had appreciated. If the currencies lost value relative to the dollar, they had depreciated. Countries were at liberty to manage the exchange rates of their currencies to the dollar at will. The system worked well for 28 years.

During the period from 1930 to 1973 foreign exchange transactions were executed internally by banks which had multiple customers buying and selling currencies daily. In addition, there were a number of independent foreign exchange trading firms, which bought and sold currencies on behalf of their clients, maintaining confidentiality and orderly markets. Transactions were executed verbally over the phone, and electronically via a telex, which was a mechanical device operated much like a typewriter, sending messages over telephone lines and transoceanic cables. Written confirmations were sent via telex and mail. Such a system, as you can imagine, had severe limitations both with respect to time, with significant lags, and volume. There was a limited capacity for the number of transactions.

Because of diminishing trade surpluses, and accumulating balance of payments deficits, in 1973 the United States was forced to abandon the gold standard, and with it, so did the rest of the world. At that time, the freely floating exchange rate system was implemented. In effect, without reference to gold, exchange rates were determined by the laws of supply and demand. When currencies lost value relative to another currency, a currency had depreciated. Conversely, if a currency gained value, it had appreciated. Governments could allow the markets to determine rates of exchange, or they could, as frequently happened, intervene by buying or selling a currency to maintain a stable market. There are many factors which influence markets and exchange rates. Those factors include volume of trade, individual country economic performance, interest rates, expectations, and unanticipated events.

How well do floating exchange rate systems work?

By and large the floating exchange rate system works very well. One notable exception occurred in 1992 when George Soros, a prominent financier, was convinced that the British pound was overvalued. He sold 10 billion pounds short, which is to say that he contracted to deliver pounds at a future date without owning or holding the pounds at the time that he entered into the transaction. Indeed, the Bank of England was forced to devalue the pound and Mr. Soros earned over $1 billion for his gamble/perception.

There are many strong currencies in the world. Among them are the Swiss franc, the Hong Kong dollar, the Australian dollar, and the Canadian dollar. However, by far the most frequently traded currencies are the United States dollar, the euro, the Japanese yen and the British pound. The Chinese yuan is creeping up in volume because of the sheer size of the Chinese economy, which is now the world's second largest. Because, as noted, the United States is the largest economy in the world, the dollar has dominated global exchange markets for decades. The euro, a currency shared by 19 European countries which make up the European Monetary Union, is second, and the Japanese yen, as the former second largest economy in the globe, is the third.

Important economic and political events have influenced the global exchange systems. Japan entered a period of prolonged economic malaise in 1990. The twenty-nine-year period of relative economic stagnation has required intervention by the Bank of Japan and other central banks to maintain currency stability. The euro as a single European currency did not exist until 1999. The stability and continued reliance on the United States dollar has been under fire for many years because of the ongoing trade deficit, dating back to 1976.

Modern technology, the use of computers, satellite systems, data processing and communications has facilitated the vast increase in global trade, investment, and volume of foreign currency transactions. Lag times have all but been eliminated as have any limitations to the volume and frequency of transactions. In fact, if anything, modern technology now allows those with access to the best of technology to enter and exit the market in nanoseconds, capturing instant profits while others linger by on the sidelines.

What is the status of the floating exchange rate system?

As a mainstay of the system, stability of the dollar is important. That policy is not necessarily consistent with the best interests of the United States. A stable or appreciating dollar makes United States exports expensive and foreign imports cheap. That is because a strong dollar buys more of a foreign currency for less and thus enables cheap imports to increase in sales. On the other hand, the cost to foreigners to purchase dollars is high, thus making it expensive to purchase

United States goods and services. This problem exacerbates the already seriously difficult challenge of diminishing the United States trade deficit. Nevertheless, international exchange markets continue to be quite orderly and stable.

Threatening market stability is the fact that as a once powerful creditor nation, the United States is now a very reliant debtor nation. In point of fact, this issue should be subdivided into two parts:

Foreign investments in the United States and United States investments abroad, which are a part of ongoing business transactions.

The sale of government obligations to foreign investors to sustain positive financial capital inflows to offset our trade deficits.

The flow of international investments is an outgrowth of inter-market dependency. Multinational corporations and investors are keenly interested in optimizing profit opportunities in domestic as well as foreign markets. This allows for building increased market share for selling goods and services, and it provides for greater diversification against market shifts and changing business cycles.

Because of increasing federal budget deficits and the resulting increase in the national debt, the United States government has become increasingly reliant on foreign governments to invest in United States Treasury obligations. Of late, the largest foreign government investor in United States Treasury obligations has been China. This has been the result of the development of a codependent relationship. As China has sought to increase its GDP, it has used its export sector as the major driver. To accomplish this, China has relied disproportionately on the United States market to sell its exports. It may sound like circular reasoning, and indeed it is, that the Chinese are in fact financing their own exports by purchasing United States Treasuries. The question arises, how long can this process continue?

Essentials of Macroeconomics

The Bank for International Settlements (BIS) was organized in 1930 to foster international monetary and financial cooperation. As of 2020, there were 60 member countries from Europe, Asia, Africa and North America. In addition to serving as a clearing house and counterparty to central banks, BIS establishes and regulates capital/asset ratios for major international banks throughout the world. The purpose of this supervisory role is to assure capital adequacy among banks whose financial activities are an integral part of global finance.

The International Monetary Fund (IMF) was formed in 1945 as part of the initiatives taken in Bretton Woods. As of 2020, there were 189 member countries. In addition to fostering monetary and financial stability, similar to that of BIS, the IMF promotes high employment, sustainable economic growth and reduction in poverty. Focusing on balance of payment issues, the IMF receives funding from member countries and provides financial assistance in the form of loans to countries encountering serious balance of payment deficits.

What are the international organizations which provide economic assistance and fund economic development?

The principal organization that provides economic assistance is the International Bank for Reconstruction and Development (the World Bank). It was organized in 1944 with the express purpose of fighting poverty. The 189 members of the World Bank). The World Bank provides financial assistance for capital intensive or infrastructure projects in developing countries.

There are a number of regional development banks, which carry on activities similar to the World Bank. They are:

- The Inter- American Development Bank
- The African Development Bank
- The Central American Bank for Economic Integration

- Asian Development Bank

- European Bank for Reconstruction and Development

- CAF Development Bank of Latin America

- European Investment Bank

This list is not all-inclusive. Major private international banks, located in the world's financial centers, provide loans and services to promote economic growth and support investment, trade, and financial activities of both the private and public sectors.

Summary

International finance, the funding of trade and investment transactions, has been a critical part of the evolution of global integration. To perform efficiently and effectively, financial entities, be they private banks, central banks, or other financial entities, require a stable global foreign exchange trading system. Essential to a stable system is currency stability. For many years a gold standard was used to provide a reference value to a currency. Those countries participating in such a system were able to advance their trading capability, while those who did not participate lingered behind. Wars interrupted the smooth development of trade, and the introduction of the International Monetary Fund in 1945 led to over twenty-five years of market growth and stability. Subsequently, it has been in the voluntary best interests of major trading nations to perfect an efficiently functioning freely floating foreign exchange system. Under such a system both the private and public sectors have been able to trade and invest internationally with minimum foreign exchange convertibility risk.

Moral Dilemmas

1.   Do currency speculators profit at the expense of firms and individuals in a country?

2.   Do people who live in countries with weak currencies become victims of actions taken by governments and central banks of countries with strong currencies?

3.   How do people, private and public entities in poor or underdeveloped countries attract capital to finance growth and development?

Moral Commentary

1.   The world of international finance is a high stakes arena. Just as is the case of strong firms attracting capital in domestic markets, strong nations, with stable economies and low risk factors attract capital at low cost, while weaker nations with volatile economies and high risk have difficulty attracting capital even at higher costs. What, if any, are the responsibilities of strong nations to reach out and stimulate growth and stability in weaker nations?

2.   Twenty-seven countries comprise the European Union of which 19 have adopted a common currency, the euro. Unlike the United States, a republic of 50 states with both a common currency and federal or nationwide fiscal policy, the 19 euro currency nations have independent fiscal policies. The economies of those nations vary from the strong and stable, such as France or Germany to the fragile and unstable, such as Italy, Spain and Greece. What, if any, are the responsibilities of the stronger, wealthier nations to provide financial assistance to member nations that experience economic hardship?

3.   To finance infrastructure and economic development countries issue long-term debts. Their bonds typically have maturities ranging from ten to thirty years. If the issuing countries experience strong economic performance and are current in servicing their debts, the bonds maintain their market value. However, over the life of the bonds, some countries experience economic challenges and interruption in debt service; sometimes even to the point of outright default. Should

these countries be entitled to some economic or debt relief? If speculators have purchased bonds at deep discounts, that is significantly less than 100 cents on the dollar, should such speculators be allowed to profit by demanding payment in full?

Chapter 15: Economic Fluctuations

Now that we have a context in which to measure economic behavior, we can examine causes and consequences of increases and decreases in GDP and its component factors. Back in the 1990s, after an extended period of economic growth, some economists had the audacity to raise the question, "Is the business cycle dead?" The implication was that economists, capitalists and legislators had finally figured out how to manage a constantly improving economy. A mini-recession in 2001 and a whopping big recession between 2007 and 2009 brought that fantasy to a roaring halt.

Here are some magic words that concern economists, businesspeople, government professionals, and consumers:

Like	Dislike
Certainty	Uncertainty
Predictable	Unpredictable
Expected	Unexpected
Probable	Improbable
Factual	Speculative
Stability	Instability

Essentials of Macroeconomics

What are economic fluctuations?

Perhaps it would be worthwhile defining what constitutes a successful economy. A successful economy might be defined as one in which all of the factors of production are utilized to their optimum capacity and results in an increase in output, which (1) is more rapid than the increase in population; (2) meets the wants and needs of a greater percentage of the population; and (3) provides for a general increase in the quality of life of society as a whole.

In the context of the above, simply put, fluctuations are deviations from desired results. Economic fluctuations are variations in the business cycle that impede economic progress. There is no magic formula to cure the dynamic changes in a market economy. Increases and decreases or expansion and contraction of gross domestic product are normal phenomena. The function of economists is to mitigate or minimize the impact of these fluctuations on the overall economy.

What is a business cycle?

A key factor in evaluating economic performance is the business cycle. In essence, the business cycle is a description of a period of time over which an economy declines or GDP decreases from a peak until that economy recovers to reach its former high level of output and perhaps surpasses that level to reach another optimum point.

The phases of a business cycle are: Peak. Recession. Trough. Recovery, Expansion. The peak is that maximum or optimum level of output reached before GDP begins to decrease. Recession is a phase during which the economy or GDP is decreasing. Economists define a recession as that phase in the business cycle during which GDP has decreased for two consecutive quarters. Trough, as in the case of a ditch, is the bottom of the business cycle, marked by a reversal of trends, or an increase in GDP. Recovery is that phase in which the economy is restored to the previous peak or level of output. Expansion is the period following the recovery, during which the business cycle is expanding as measured by growth or increase in output and GDP, to a new optimum level of output.

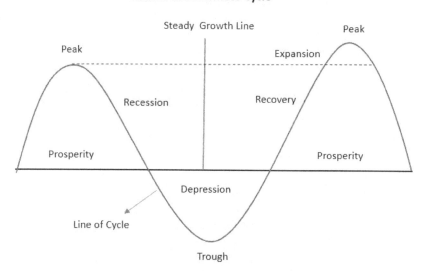

Phases of a Business Cycle

Much as economists would like to be able to predict the exact timing of the business cycle, the phases are all seen through the rearview mirror. Factors contributing to the business cycle can be well explained, but the ability to predict a business cycle precisely continues to elude economists.

As indicated in the chart below, three generalizations can be safely made. One, the frequency and volatility of business cycles decreased significantly after WWII. Two, with less volatility in the business cycles, during the period from 1962 to 2018, over the fifty-six-year period, the United States economy grew thirty-three-fold, in nominal terms, from $604 billion to $20.4 trillion. Third during that same period the population of the United States merely increased 1.75-fold, increasing from 186 million to 327 million. The phenomena can be attributed to a much more profound understanding of the causes underlying business cycles and a vast increase in the amount of economic information available to measure the cycles and to initiate remedial actions.

What are some of the theories describing business cycles?

The theories are divided into two approaches: Endogenous and Exogenous. An endogenous theory is one that examines internal causes or those factors which occur within the economic structure or framework. An exogenous theory is one that examines external causes or those which occur outside of the economic structure of framework.

Examples of endogenous theories are: Technological advances which might result in new products or new processes of production; conversely, the end of a product life might lead to decreased output and lower employment; consumer confidence, which is a highly psychological and subjective factor, can have either a positive or negative influence on economic behavior; monetary theories evolve about responses to expected levels of inflation and actions taken to increase or decrease economic activity; finally, the process of satisfying consumer demand is volatile in and of itself. Manufacturers do not know exactly what quantities of a product to produce. Consequently, the economy goes through periods of overproduction and under-production, each of which contributes to business cycle fluctuations.

Examples of exogenous theories are: The effect on the United States economy of events or actions occurring in other world economies. In recent times, the Chinese have initiated or implemented actions to promote the sale of their products in the United States. The initiation of military action in the face of a perceived threat, such as was the case in Iraq, Afghanistan, and Libya, is another example. The formation of the Organization of Petroleum Export Countries (OPEC), an initiative to manage and coordinate oil production in 1973 caused a significant setback to the United States economy then, and for many years thereafter.

Can business cycles be forecasted?

For years economists have endeavored to forecast business cycles. When do they begin? What causes an economic downturn or recession? How deep will the recession be? How long will it last? What will cause a reversal or economic recovery and when will it begin? All of these questions have evaded concrete answers. Nevertheless, there are economic indices or indicators that are accurate and reliable for what they measure. The problem lies in the relationship of the indicators and the fact that they do not necessarily coincide in their respective indications.

Of the ten leading economic indicators, let us examine four in greater detail:

- Average work week of production workers in manufacturing: An increase in the average work week would suggest an increase in output. This might suggest an increase in demand, or it might suggest a replenishment of inventories. Likewise, a decline in the average work week might suggest that demand has decreased or that inventories remain relatively high. In either event, more information is required.

- New orders for consumer goods and materials: If new orders are increasing, there is a definite indication that demand is increasing. Why? Have old products worn out? Has new technology created an increase in demand? Has population or disposable income increased? If new orders are decreasing, are consumers using products for longer periods of time? Has the population growth slowed? Has disposable income declined? Once again, more information is required.

- New orders for capital goods: Capital goods are plant and equipment used to manufacture final goods. An increase in orders for capital goods is a strong indication that owners and managers of firms manufacturing final goods have strong convictions that consumer demand will endure or increase. On the other hand, if interest rates are very low, investors are more likely to borrow and invest in plant and equipment in anticipation of an eventual increase in demand.

- New building permits issued: Building permits are required to construct industrial, commercial and residential units. Because of the lag time between obtaining a permit and completion of construction, an increase in permits is a medium-term indicator. Because housing is the largest single component of consumer expenditures, an increase in residential home construction might be a strong lead indicator of improving economic conditions. Certainly, a decrease in the number of permits issued is a strong negative indicator.

All of which is to say, that the leading economic indicators must be examined in depth to appreciate the significance of a change in numbers. As one can imagine, individual economists will attach different degrees of importance to a change in any one or several indicators.

How large is the US labor force?

With a population of 328 million inhabitants, approximately 160 million are men and women who are over the age of 16, are both mentally and physically able to perform productive work and are not incarcerated or serving military duty.

Relating to this definition is the measure of the Labor Force Participation Rate (LFPR). With a significant number of women entering the workforce between 1962 and 2000, (48% of total workforce) the LFPR peaked in 2000 at 67.3%. It has since declined to less than 63%.

What is the importance of unemployment?

After the great depression and the conclusion of WWII, there were many discussions about the role of employment in the U.S. economy. After all, of the three tangible economic resources, land, labor, and capital, the one which is most important for overall economic well-being is labor, or employment. After WWII, Congress was of a mind to charge the Executive Branch with the responsibility of guaranteeing workers employment. When it became apparent that this was neither feasible nor practical, the mandate changed to that of maximizing employment opportunities.

Employment might be defined as the measure of those members of the labor force who choose to work and are gainfully occupied or working. Conversely, unemployment is defined as those in the labor force who are without a job and are willing, able and actively seeking a new job.

The formula for measuring unemployment is:

Essentials of Macroeconomics

Unemployment rate =

Number unemployed/Labor force (measured as those employed and those unemployed)

Unfortunately, those in the labor force who are no longer seeking work, for whatever reason, and those who are under-employed, that is working fewer hours or performing work below their respective skill level are not included in the unemployment statistic.

In 2020, the size of the United States labor force was 160 million. The number encompasses those with varying levels of education, skills\, and experience. It does not distinguish among gender, race, ethnicity, religion or national origin. It does not include those who have entered the country illegally or remained here illegally.

Who are the unemployed?

Unemployed people are classified in four categories:

1. Frictional unemployment: People who voluntarily move in and out of jobs such as students, homemakers, or discharged military people are among those enduring frictional unemployment. Additionally, there is a period of frictional unemployment between the time that a position is made available and ultimately filled.

2. Structural unemployment: This type of unemployment is a consequence of technological change or change in demand for specific talents or skills. As happened in the case of a surge in demand for commercial aircraft, there was an increase in demand for workers skilled in aircraft assembly. Likewise, with the continuing advancement in computer applications, there has been increase in demand for those with computer skills. Until such demand is satisfied, there is structural unemployment.

3. Cyclical unemployment: As the business cycle expands, there is an increase in employment opportunities. Likewise, during a recession the number of positions decreases causing an increase in unemployment. During the last economic recovery in 2002 and in the current economic recovery the lag time for finding new employment opportunities has increased significantly. Increased productivity, new technology, and reduced consumption all seem to aggravate this problem.

4. Seasonal unemployment: Many industries are subject to changes in demand for goods and services during the course of the year. Such industries are: agriculture, garments, recreation, and equipment, to name a few. Those who choose to work in these industries know that from time-to-time they will be laid off, only to return to work once demand recurs.

What is inflation?

The technical definition is: Inflation is an increase in the general level of prices of goods and services. It can also be defined as a loss in purchasing power of a currency such that it takes more of the currency to purchase goods and services today, than it did one or several years ago. Like death and taxes, inflation seems to be with us eternally.

A simple explanation of the phenomenon of inflation might be the following. Back in chapter three we described price equilibrium as a point where supply and demand converge and at which both consumer and supplier are satisfied to purchase and sell a good or service. In addition, we suggested that this equilibrium point is reached through a process of trial and error.

Now, imagine that consumers converge on a particular product and the supplier does not have sufficient supplies to meet the demand. What will happen to the price of the product? It will increase. In and of itself, this does not constitute inflation. But, if the surge in demand occurs for many products at the same time, then price inflation will occur. Likewise, if for some unpredictable reason, the supply of many products is curtailed or decreased, while the demand is sustained, then inflation will also occur.

U.S. Inflation Rate Since 1914

Effective Federal Funds Rate

For the past twenty years, inflation has hovered at rates below 2.5%. For many people, this makes the concept of inflation difficult to comprehend. From year-to-year, at that level, what $100 will purchase today will require $102.50 a year from today. That seems like a very small decrease in purchasing power. Look back to 1983 when that same $100 at the beginning of the year required $115 to purchase the same good or service one year later.

How is inflation measured?

The Consumer Price Index (CPI) has been the standard measure of inflation. An index is a measure of a number on a scale. Indices require a base line or fixed reference number against which quantities or numbers are compared. Indices can measure standards, performance or trends.

Essentials of Macroeconomics

The CPI is determined by a market basket of goods and services which represent the typical consumption patterns of U.S. families. For example, the market basket includes food, clothing, rent, utilities, auto expenses, appliances, including personal computers, and travel and entertainment expenses. The market basket is modified from time-to-time to reflect changes in consumption. Surely, it will not be too long before iPads are included.

The formula for measuring a change In the CPI is:

Percent increase in CPI =

(CPI in current year – CPI in previous year)/CPI previous year

The current base year of the CPI is 1983 with the base number being 100. In June 2020, the index was 258. That is an average compound rate of 2.58 per annum.

What are deflation and disinflation?

If inflation is defined as an increase in the general level of prices of goods and services. Then it is logical that deflation would be defined as a decrease in the general level of prices of goods and services. Just as inflation tends to be a trend over several years, deflation also tends to be a trend enduring several years. Likewise, one could define deflation as an increase in the purchasing power of a currency. Economists have mixed thoughts about the effects of deflation. While it is clear that consumers benefit from the increased purchasing power of their disposable income, producers and distributors lose money because they are selling goods and services for less than the cost of production and delivery. Over a period of time the costs of resources must be adjusted downward, meaning reduced salaries and wages, as well as reduced costs of raw materials and other inputs. As one can imagine, wage earners are very reluctant to accept reduced income.

Essentials of Macroeconomics

Disinflation is a reduction in the rate of increase of inflation. During the period immediately after WWII, when there was pent-up demand for housing, automobiles and consumer goods, inflation increased rapidly. Once the manufacturing sector converted from producing war materials to those of peacetime, supply fell more in line with demand, and the rate of inflation declined rapidly.

Who is hurt by inflation and who is helped?

Three groups of people stand out as suffering the most during periods of inflation. The first group is the poor whose income level is low to begin with and does not increase at a sufficient rate to keep up with rising prices. The second group is those people, typically retirees, who depend on fixed income. They, too, cannot keep up with rising prices. The final group is lenders who have extended credit at fixed rates for long periods. The money with which they are repaid has less purchasing power than the money which they loaned.

Three groups of people tend to benefit from inflation. The first group is the rich because the portion of their income spent on consumption is less than that of other groups. Their ability to maintain their level of living is least threatened. The second group is debtors who have borrowed money at fixed rates for long periods and are repaying their loans with cheaper dollars. The final group is business owners who are able to sell inventories acquired at lower prices for higher prices.

In a sense, the above is a simplification of the disadvantaged and advantaged by inflation. The ability of lenders and businesspeople to adjust prices affects the impact of inflation in varying degrees. Cost of living adjustments (COLA) built into Social Security payments and in many union wage agreements lag inflation. That is the adjustments are ex post facto (they come after the fact).

Essentials of Macroeconomics

What are demand-pull inflation and cost-push inflation?

Very simply put, when the demand for goods exceeds the supply, inflation is referred to as demand-pull. The high level of inflation immediately succeeding WWII was a classic example of demand-pull inflation. Another period when demand-pull inflation is likely to occur is at the point in the business cycle when the economy has passed through the trough and is just beginning to expand or recover. Producers will have reduced output and allowed inventories to decrease while consumers are, once again purchasing more goods and services.

Cost-push inflation occurs when wages have spiraled upwards causing an increase in the cost of goods produced, or as occurred during the1970s when the cost of oil tripled over a five-year period. This cost increase was pervasive because of its effect on transportation and petroleum-based products. Such spiraling wages have often been attributed to union wage negotiations. The reduced number of union workers in the private sector will determine whether or not this assertion holds true. A second factor is that attributable to those industries dominated by a few firms which may be able to ignore market forces and increase prices of goods and services to increase profits. Examples of such industries are tobacco, cereals, detergents, and oil. A third factor is a sudden curtailment in supply. The best example of this "supply shock" event is the 1973 reduction in oil supply imposed by the Organization of Petroleum Export Countries (OPEC). Because every product either has an oil component or requires transportation to market, the reduction in supply had a very pervasive effect on market prices.

Does inflation have a psychological effect on the population?

The answer to that question is "yes." Most populations, including that of the United States, are comfortable with a modest level of inflation, that level ranging between 2 and 5%. As the rate of inflation increases, populations become agitated and anticipate that it will continue to increase. The result is a period of uncertainty and economic instability. Consumers spend less and save more. Producers decrease output, reduce purchases of raw material and lay off workers.

What is the difference between creeping inflation and hyperinflation?

Creeping inflation is the low level of the rate of increase described above. Creeping inflation ranges from 2 to 5% over a sustained period and generally does not have a destabilizing effect. Hyperinflation is defined as an accumulated level of inflation of 120% over a three-year period. That is the equivalent of compounding 30% over a three-year period. A single year of double-digit inflation does not in and of itself constitute hyperinflation. It is the sustained hyper-level that has significant destructive consequences. Under such circumstances, currencies become worthless. People lose confidence in the currency, the government, and the economy. The most outstanding example of such destruction in recent times is that of Zimbabwe, a country which has endured a hyperinflation level of 9,000%, and more recently Venezuela, which is approaching 1,000,000%.

Summary

Economic fluctuations as measured by the business cycle, unemployment and inflation are inextricably intertwined. During periods of prosperity, when supply and demand are relatively balanced, there is likely to be full employment and price stability. During periods of a contracting economy, when supply and demand are likely to be imbalanced, there results a decrease in employment and an increased likelihood of a period of inflation. Economics is frequently defined as the study of the allocation of scarce resources to satisfy human wants. In fact, economics is much more complex than that definition implies. We charge economists with the responsibility of managing economic factors such as government spending, the money supply, forces affecting the demand and supply of goods and services, inflation and employment so as to create a stable and sustainable economy. As we move into the next chapter, we shall review how some economists have theorized about such issues.

Moral Dilemmas

1.   During an economic recession some sectors, firms, and individuals suffer more than others. Should either the private or public sector take measures to immunize or provide relief for those who suffer disproportionately?

2.   Structural unemployment occurs as a result of technological change and some skills become obsolete. Should the private or public sectors provide relief, re-education, or retraining to enable workers to stay in the workforce?

3.   Seasonal workers are particularly important in the agriculture sector. Should there be regulations and financial relief for those whose work by definition is short-term, transitory, and geographically dispersed?

4.   Both lenders and savers lose with the diminished purchasing power of money repaid or savings built over long periods of time. Should there be instruments or mechanisms by which these financial losses are immunized against such losses?

5.   Because of inflation, through no effort or initiative on their part, borrowers are able to repay their debts with cheaper dollars. Those merchants with accumulated inventories are able to reprice their merchandise to avoid financial losses. Should these unearned benefits be enjoyed unencumbered by tax or regulation?

Moral Commentary

1.   During periods of contraction in the business cycle, firms, suffering from decreased demands for their goods and services, lay off workers. More often than not, those most threatened with job loss are semi-skilled and skilled workers. With low wages and lack of health benefits, unemployment insurance provides minimal relief. Should or should not state and federal governments provide affordable and

accessible health insurance and more generous unemployment relief? Would programs encouraging or stimulating shared wage and salary reductions be more equitable?

2.   Business cycles do not affect all industries, all sectors of the economy and all geographic parts of the country uniformly. This was as true during the great depression of the 1930s as it was of the great recession of 2007 through 2009. For firms, the ability to endure short and long-term declines or business threats in levels of cash maintained and on the strength of their balance sheets, particularly their equity. Similarly, the ability of individuals and households to sustain difficult periods is reflected in minimizing debt and maximizing savings. What, if any, action or programs might a government offer to those firms and or families least prepared to overcome economic threats?

Chapter 16: Income Distribution and Poverty

The population of the United States is 328 million. Of this total, 10% or 32 million live at or below the poverty level, which is defined as 3 times the cost of three nutritional meals per day. For a family of four that number is $26 thousand. In a country with per capita income of $54 thousand, there arise many questions about the distribution of income; how to support those permanently or temporarily impoverished, who should provide those services and how to pay for those services. Understanding both the causes and consequences of poverty is essential to developing solutions to the problems of poverty.

How is income distributed in the United States?

Why is the discussion of the distribution of income an important topic? Those countries which have prospered the most throughout history have been those with an upwardly mobile labor force, with respect for private property, with freely competitive markets, and with effective educational systems. In addition, especially since WWII, the United States economy has been very dependent on consumer spending to drive economic growth.

The United States Census Bureau divides income into five brackets called quintiles. Let's look at a few numbers to examine not only the current distribution of income, but also the trends that have occurred over the past sixty years.

Year	Population (M)	Percent of Total Income by Quintile				
		1st	2d	3rd	4th	5th
1947	150	5.0	11.9	17.0	23.1	43.0
1969	203	5.6	12.4	17.7	23.7	40.5
1989	248	4.6	10.5	16.5	23.7	44.5
2009	298	3.4	8.6	14.5	23.2	50.3
2014	320	3.1	8.2	14.3	23.2	51.2
2017	324	3.1	8.2	14.3	23.0	51.3

For the first twenty-five years after WWII the statistics reflect a trend of the distribution of income favoring the poor and the middle class, quintile 1 being the lowest and quintiles 2, 3, and 4 representing the middle-income groups. The distribution in the top 20%, the fifth quintile dropped from 43% to 40%. Then the trend reversed. The lowest 20% decreased to 3.1% and all three middle income groups decreased by a total of 15%. The upper 20% increased their share of total income by 27%.

Just out of curiosity, let's look at another set of numbers. What were the upper levels of real (000 dollars) income for households in each of the income brackets referred to above?

Essentials of Macroeconomics

Year	Percent of Total Income by Quintile				
	1st	2d	3rd	4th	5th
1969	9.7	18.6	26.8	37.6	58.9
1989	9.8	18.4	28.3	43.0	73.4
2009	9.5	17.9	28.6	46.3	83.3
2014	21.4	41.2	68.2	112.3	206.2
2017	24.6	47.1	77.6	126.9	237.0

How does income distribution in the United States compare with other countries?

M. O. Lorenz created a graphic depiction of this distribution. Called the Lorenz curve, it contrasts the actual distribution of income against a hypothetical perfect distribution. The "y" axis measures percent of total income. The "x" axis measures percent of households. The hypothetical perfect distribution falls on the 45° line which bisects the graph. The degree of separation of the Lorenz Curve from the 45° line indicates that there is a greater disparity in the distribution of income.

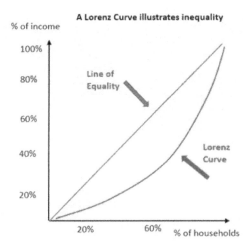

The Lorenz Curve graphically demonstrates the difference between perfect distribution and actual distribution. The Gini Index, which measures income distribution, quantifies that difference. For example, a country with perfect distribution would be a "0" on the Gini Index. A country in which one person received all the income, and the remaining population nothing would be a "1" on the index. The following table gives some examples for sake of comparison. The dates are inconsistent, but the trends all reflect a 30-year period.

Year	US	Bangladesh	Brazil	China	Russia	Germany
1988+	37.5	28.8	61.4	na	46.1	29.2
2015+	41.5	32.4	51.3	42.8	37.7	31.7

Bangladesh is a poverty-stricken country in south-east Asia. The index has changed very little. Brazil is an emerging economy with substantial resources. As its economy has expanded and its population increased, income distribution has improved. Between 1988 and 2015, Russia lost significant territory and population. Its economy has contracted and its dependence on oil and gas has caused substantial upheaval in the country. The result seems to indicate some improvement in income distribution. There is more to that story. In the case of the United States, income distribution has deteriorated.

Should there be an equal distribution of income among all people?

Should those who work hard be rewarded more than others? Should those who have special talents earn more than others? Should people with large families be paid more than those with small families? Should older people with more experience be paid more than younger people who may have more energy? All of these questions present value judgments, which only you as the student can determine.

Further complicating the unequal distribution of income is the unequal distribution of household income among races. In the United States, the average household income for white families is $68 thousand (K), while that of Blacks is $40K, Hispanics $50K and Asians $81K. Even with these disparities, in general the standards of living have improved for all categories over the past 60 years.

When addressing the distribution of income on a global basis the mal-distribution or inequality is even worse. Of a world population of more than seven billion people, about 700 million live on less than $2 per day. This is a significant improvement over twenty years ago when 2 billion or almost 30% lived in abject poverty. The top 20% consume 86% of all goods and services and the bottom 20% barely 5%.

As you can imagine, a corollary to unequal income distribution is the distribution of wealth. Income represents a cash flow while wealth represents an accumulation of income or storage of assets. Every year *Forbes Magazine* publishes a list of the world's wealthiest people. We all know the names of Jeff Bezos, Bill Gates and Warren Buffett, but who would imagine that, out of one single investment in Wal-Mart, four Waltons would be among the ten wealthiest people. Outside of the United States, there is Carlos Slim of Mexico, and, more recently, individuals from Russia and China (PRC) have entered the list of world billionaires.

Globally, there is no single standard of values regarding the distribution of income or wealth. Different societies treat the issue with different solutions. Among the Scandinavian countries and in Germany and France income redistribution is very high because people look to the government to provide extensive cradle to grave services. Emerging nations, such as Brazil, China and India tend to have extreme differences between the rich and the poor, and a lack of public services. Capitalist countries lie somewhere in between.

In the United States the notion of redistribution of income has been embedded in the income tax code since 1862, when the income tax was introduced by the Union to finance the Civil War. During the 1960s the highest marginal tax rate reached 91%. The marginal tax declined to 70% during the 1970s, to 50% in the 1980s, and in 2020 the highest marginal tax rate is 35%. There is an ongoing national debate about the justification of taxing high income earners to a greater degree than middle class income earners.

What determines income distribution?

There are three determinants of income distribution:

1. Wages and salaries reflect differences in income attributable to intelligence, skill, experience, education, and training. Wages are incomes earned based on hourly or output performance. Salaries are incomes earned on a weekly monthly or annual basis.

2. Property income is the rent, interest or profits generated by accumulated wealth. The wealth itself might be personally generated or inherited, but in either case is the result of an initial level of high income.

3. Income from government transfer programs is referred to as unearned income that is paid to provide relief or a cushion against impoverishment. Whether it is Social Security paid to retirees or the disabled, welfare programs such as Medicaid or food stamps paid to those with low incomes, these transfer payments are made to provide temporary or permanent support.

Who are the poor in America?

Relative to Bill Gates or Warren Buffett, one could say that we are all poor. On the other hand, relative to those two million people living on less than $2 per day, we are all rich. So! How do we define poverty in the United States? Should poverty be defined by level of income, or by the level of consumption? Is the poverty level the same in Hawaii as in Oklahoma, the highest and lowest states as measured by cost of living? Is poverty different for those who have access to nutritional food, sanitary conditions and good health treatment versus those denied such benefits?

As mentioned at the beginning of this chapter, the United States Census Bureau defines poverty as that level of income which is three times the cost of three nutritional meals per day. This formula has remained unchanged in spite of the fact that the cost of food has declined over the past fifty years. As indicated by the chart in the text, the portion of the population living in poverty has declined from a level of 23% in 1959 to 13% in 2017.

In absolute numbers, most poor people are white. However, when the numbers are analyzed relative to the composition of the population, among blacks the percentage of poor people is higher than among whites, Hispanics, or Asians. It is a misconception to think that most of the poor are concentrated in the inner cities. Yes! Detroit, New York, Chicago and Cleveland have large poor populations, but so do Kansas, South Dakota, Alabama and Mississippi.

The percentage of children who live in poverty, those under the age of 18, in the United States is among the highest of the world's wealthiest nations at 22.5%. The question worth asking is, "How many of these children escape poverty in their adulthood?" The answer, unfortunately, is too few. 10.6% of those between the ages of 18 and 65 live in poverty, and 9.7% of people over the age of 65 live in poverty.

What causes people to live in poverty?

There are many misconceptions about poverty that arise out of prejudice or unchallenged assertions.

- Are the poor lazy? Aren't we all? Laziness is not a significant factor or underlying cause of poverty.

- Is the heritage of slavery a cause of poverty? How one phrases a question can significantly affect the response. A more appropriate question is whether or not systemic discrimination is a cause of poverty. The answer to the latter question is yes, whether it is discrimination based on race, nationality, creed, gender, age, sexual preference, or disability.

- Is there employment discrimination? Yes! In addition to the factors mentioned above, there is discrimination based on education, even to the point of what school did one attend, one's height, weight, and recently, the period of time spent unemployed.

Essentials of Macroeconomics

- What does it mean to be Black in America? The civil rights act of 1964 and the Voting Rights Act of 1965 were meant to cure the problem of racial inequality in the workplace, in daily life, and in education. Many would argue that, even with major inroads to the board rooms of large corporations, to more integrated housing and to higher education, there is still a large segment of the Black population that has been left behind. There is a high percentage of Black families with single mothers. There is a high percentage of Black males who are incarcerated. There is a high percentage of young Black students who drop out of school, and there continues to be discrimination in the workplace.

- Does poverty breed poverty? A more important question is, "How upwardly mobile is the American economy?" If poverty is accompanied by poor nutrition, lack of good health protection, living in endangered conditions and suffering from inadequate education, there is an increased likelihood of perpetuating poverty. What I am suggesting is that framing a question in a negative context tends to produce negative results; whereas, framing a question in a more positive or open context tends to lead to solutions.

- What is the meaning of human capital? Human capital refers to the talents, skills, and experience that an individual has accumulated and is able to contribute. A measure of the general adequacy of human capital in an economy is reflected in the number of filled or unfilled jobs that can be attributed to the talents, skills and experience of the entire workforce. This is another way to approach the structural cause of unemployment. When an economy shifts, as has the United States economy, from an industrial to a service and then to an information base, there is a period during which there is an insufficient supply of human capital to meet the change in demand.

Essentials of Macroeconomics

Since this is not a course of political science, let us confine our discussion to the economic causes, effects, problems and solutions of poverty. As we have tried to explain in this chapter, there are many underlying causes of poverty ranging from education, discrimination based on race, age, gender, or disability, family life, to society's economic and social mobility. In addition to some placing emphasis on one factor versus another, there is also a discussion about who should be provided with relief, in what form that relief should be provided, and, of course, who should pay for the relief. There are those who think that by limiting relief the poor will be goaded into working. There are those who would provide relief without concern about the ability to pay for such costs. In the end, there are no hard statistics or concrete facts to evidence that any single formula or approach achieves the desired objectives.

Solutions range from doing nothing to providing massive aid in the form of welfare, training, and job incentives. One substantiated accomplishment of the Personal Responsibility and Work Reconciliation Act of 1996 was the reduction in the number of welfare recipients from 10 million in 1996 to 4 million in 2009. This statistic quantifies the number of welfare recipients, but it does not address the standard of living of the poor.

Summary

It is difficult to have a discussion about poverty and poor people in a substantive and objective manner. Much of our beliefs and attitudes come from our own personal upbringing and our early-life exposures to poor people. Poverty exists throughout our economy racially, demographically by age and gender, and geographically. The causes of poverty range from situation at birth, access to adequate health services, education, and discrimination. One topic that was not discussed was that of the role of *good luck*. A uniform understanding of causes and solutions to poverty does not exist. One traditional approach has been a progressive tax system, which is coming under scrutiny increasingly, every day. The latest attempt at a solution, the Personal Responsibility and Work

Reconciliation Act of 1996 has had definitive quantitative results, but not measurable qualitative results.

Moral Dilemmas

1.   Does a developed, wealthy nation have a different responsibility to provide relief to the under privileged than an underdeveloped, poor nation?

2.   Is there a moral limit to income and wealth accumulation relative to the general population?

3.   If opportunities are provided and not availed, does there continue to be a responsibility to provide relief?

4.   What ought to be the roles of both the private and public sectors?

5.   What are the effects of greed, cronyism, and kleptocracy on income distribution and wealth accumulation?

Moral Commentary

1.   The word *zombie* has been coined to define individuals or groups who continue to pursue or implement policies claiming that the policies will produce results long proven not to work. For example, reducing taxes on wealthy individuals or families with the expectation that the increase in disposable income will cause an increase in both consumption and investment. In addition, the resulting increase in GDP will contribute to an increase in tax revenue to offset the reduction in taxes. Relative to the lost tax revenue, neither consumption nor investment increases. Furthermore, during post WWII periods, marginal income tax rates reached 90% and economic growth continued unabated. What is the impact on income distribution and wealth of these policies? What measures, if any, ought to be introduced to avoid these *zombie* advocated policies?

2.   The developed countries with lower Gini indices or income distribution more closely approximating the equality line on the Lorenz Curve, Germany, Norway, Sweden, and Denmark, to name a few, have much more homogeneous populations than the US. The willingness to provide cradle to grave public services in what may appropriately be characterized as a more socialized economy is both a reflection of economic choices and cultural preferences. Conversely, in the United States, such socialistic policies are characterized as being contrary to our capitalistic, free market economy and perceived to be unproductive. The question arises, is the difference between an homogeneous population versus an heterogeneous population a cause of different approaches to public policy decision making, or is it a correlation?

Chapter 17: The Mixed Economy

Is the United States economy capitalistic, or something else?

The United States is referred to as a capitalist system in which private property, free private enterprise, the price mechanism, and unfettered, competitive markets prevail. Yet, our economy is also a mixed economy. What does that mean? In fact, there are two sectors of the economy; the private sector, which refers to individual citizens' ownership of firms and the means of production, and the public sector, which refers to federal, state and local government entities.

In order to solve the economic problem of how to allocate scarce resources to satisfy insatiable wants, three primary questions are asked:

1. What shall we produce? That is, shall we produce many, diverse goods and products, or just a few? Shall we increase the production of services or not? Shall we increase the production of the private sector or that of the public sector? Within this question is a sub-question, which is, who should determine what to produce, consumers, producers, or the government?

2. How shall these goods and services be produced? That question is directed at the use of resources. Do we want to dedicate more land to oil and gas exploration? Do we want to divert water to build hydroelectric

dams? Do we want to use more land for urban development? Do we want more labor-intensive industries or capital-intensive industries? How do we optimize the skills of our labor force and opportunities for employment? How do we want to optimize the use of technology? This question also has an embedded sub-question: How are resources made available to produce goods and services, via a competitive market or via government allocation?

3. For whom shall the goods and services be produced? Should all goods and services be equally available to all consumers (non-rivalry), or should some services be available to all and some only to those who can pay for them (excludable)? What goods and services are in the general publics' best interest to be universally available (non-rivalry)? Should some goods or services be denied (rivalry) or made prohibitively expensive (excludable)?

How are the objectives of the private sector distinguished from those of the public sector?

The mixed economy is based on the concepts of rivalry and excludability. Rivalry is the notion that there are insufficient goods to satisfy all consumers. Therefore, what one consumer obtains is, by definition, denied to another, because there are insufficient goods and services to satisfy the entire demand. Excludability is the notion that one has to pay for a good or service to obtain it. Both of these concepts form the essence of free private enterprise and open competition. Manufacturers and producers of goods and services purposely do not provide enough to satisfy all consumers. That is how prices are influenced. When there are more consumers seeking a good than there is a good available, prices will rise. Conversely, if there are more goods or services available than the aggregate demand, prices will fall.

On the other hand, it is in the public interest that some services be equally available to all, non-rivalry, and available without regard to cost or price, non-excludable. Such goods and services are provided by the public sector, where there is no profit motive. For example, it is in the public interest that all enjoy police and fire protection; that all benefit from street and highway access; that all enjoy public parks. The establishment of a universal system of justice and a national defense organization are also among these non-rivalry and non-excludability services.

Sometimes referred to as "the father of economics," what did Adam Smith contribute?

Adam Smith was a prominent articulator of how a free private enterprise system should function. In 1776, at the time of the American Revolution, he coined a term, "The invisible hand." It must be appreciated that Adam Smith was a humanist and believed in the fundamental goodness of mankind. In his concept, the entrepreneur, that is leaders and creators of business enterprises were motivated by self-interest. That, in spite of having no interest in promoting the public interest, his/her actions, over time, indeed would come to serve the public interest. How does this work? Imagine that an entrepreneur decides to make profits by manufacturing iPads. This enterprise requires plant and equipment, technology, raw materials, and labor. By engaging all of these resources, the entrepreneur is serving the public interest. Furthermore, in the pursuit of even greater profits, the entrepreneur must lower costs and pass on the savings in the form of lower prices, thus, once again, serving the public good.

In today's markets, Smith's concept may appear naïve. The concentration of power in large, oligopolistic industries combined with human greed frequently puts in question whether or not the public interest is being well-served.

Essentials of Macroeconomics

What is the price mechanism?

The price mechanism is the guiding principle underpinning the free market system. High prices drive away customers and low prices attract customers. If one producer, through optimum use of resources, land, labor and capital, can sell a product at a low price, all producers of that good are forced to sell at the same or lower price. If a producer's costs are too high to compete, then that producer will fail and go out of business. This failure results in a decrease in the supply of that product in the market. With increased scarcity and the same continued level of demand, the remaining producer(s) realize increased profits from higher selling prices. If such higher profit levels are sustained, then new producers will enter the market, supply will increase and prices will decrease. Thus, it is that prices drive the marketplace and, in turn, determine the allocation of resources.

What is a market?

A market is a place, physical or virtual, where independent buyers and sellers are free to enter and exit at will. In this market, multiple firms or enterprises may offer the same goods or services without restriction. This convergence of firms offering the same or similar goods and services is competition. Survivors in this free market are those who can offer their goods or services at the lowest prices, and at least break-even costs. Price is not always the determining factor. Consumers are often attracted by non-price offers such as convenience, distinct quality, and guaranties.

Trust and Equity are two principles that apply universally and are beyond the scope of economics. In that context, *trust* and *equity* are as essential to an efficient and sustainable economic system as they are to the relationships between and among people.

Trust is a mutual understanding between two parties: That each is acting in good faith; That neither party is withholding information or attempting to deceive or take advantage of the other; That each party will fulfill his/her responsibilities in a bargain, as promised.

Equity is the quality of being fair, just, and impartial.

For an economic system to function efficiently, smoothly, and enduringly, it is important that individuals enter into transactions with a high degree of trust. Failure to uphold the element of trust leads to systemic failure. Likewise, the element of equity is important. If, in addition to upholding trust, there is also a sense of fairness, then the system thrives. The moment either of these two factors is placed in jeopardy, the system breaks down and/or fails.

Will firms act in a manner to create trust and equity to serve their own best interests?

In the United States economy, the vast majority of transactions are executed with trust and equity. People buy and sell goods and services expecting that each party is acting in good faith and that there is a fair exchange of value. Nevertheless, as reflected in the many federal agencies designed to regulate and enforce certain standards of behavior, there are enough individuals and institutions who fail to observe acceptable standards of performance that the government must intervene to prevent or correct their behavior. Examples include agencies such as the Food and Drug Administration, which was created to assure the production and distribution of safe medical products; the National Labor Relations Board, which was created to protect employees' ability to enjoy collective representation and adjudicate labor disputes; the Federal Deposit Insurance Corporation, which was created to insure banks and regulate transactions among banks and their customers; and the Securities and Exchange Commission, which regulates stock and bond transactions to assure prompt and public disclosure to protect investors.

Essentials of Macroeconomics

Throughout history, there has been a trend towards the concentration of power and the subsequent abuse of that power. Those societies or economies which recognize this reality deal with it through a fair judicial system and by providing a dynamic legal structure which adapts to the changing technological and market conditions.

The student should be constantly aware of the moral and ethical consequences of economic behavior and should examine economic concepts and principles in terms of their implications on firms, consumers, markets, and society.

What is an efficient market?

Efficiency is the hallmark measure of market productivity with minimum waste of resources or expense. By responding to consumer wants and needs, producers of goods and services make decisions about what combination of resources are necessary to satisfy consumers. Some decisions are brilliant, cost-effective and ensure the provision of goods and services at the lowest possible price. Some decisions are not so smart and result in inefficiencies and higher prices. In an efficiently functioning competitive market, the former succeed and the latter fail.

What is the role of the federal government to optimize an efficient market?

In the mixed economy, governments play distinctive roles. In the United States there are three levels of government: federal, state, and local. There are some services uniquely delegated to one level or the other. There are other services in which all levels may be involved. To give an example, national security is uniquely a federal government service, as are the services of many regulatory agencies such as the Food and Drug Administration, or the Department of Labor, or the Department of Commerce. Likewise, states provide civil and criminal justice systems, state police services and state highway networks. Local governments provide police, fire, and sanitation services. Judicial services are provided at all levels.

Essentials of Macroeconomics

Above all, however, the principle role of government is to provide a fair and equitable legal system, and an economically stable environment in which goods and services are traded and move freely throughout the nation. When this process enables individuals and firms to maximize their profit potential and consumers have access to goods and services at optimally low prices there is market success. When there are distortions, such as one or a few firms dominating a market, allowing for excess profits, or where consumers are denied access to free and open markets, and resources cease to be allocated efficiently, then there is market failure.

What are some indications of market failure?

Throughout history there have been externalities or spillovers. If settlers deforest the land to use wood for fires and construction, natural soil erosion occurs and nutrients are lost. The benefit of the fire and construction is reaped by one while the loss of good farmland or stable earth is borne by another. Only since the 1960s has the United States seriously incorporated the notion of externalities as an economic cost or benefit.

As you might be able to determine by the above example, an externality or spillover is the benefit or expense accrued by a third party because of the action of another. For example, if a power plant installs scrubbers on its chimneys to reduce air pollution, the benefit of clean air is enjoyed by all, even though they did not install the scrubbers. Similarly, if a chemical plant deposits waste materials in the soil or into nearby streams, the resulting consequences in the form of pollution are borne by third parties who cannot drink the water, fish in the streams, or swim in the waters.

If private enterprise does not voluntarily invest in negative externality elimination or reduction, the federal government has two options: One is to provide economic incentives such as tax relief or subsidies. The other option is to penalize through fines and imposed cleanup expenses.

When discussing the difference between the private and the public sector, we described certain types of services provided in a non-rivalry and non-excludable manner. These public services, which include national defense, maintenance of a national infrastructure, highways, airports, railways and communication systems, are essential to the smooth, stable function of the economy. A successful government is one that maintains public services that facilitate a prosperous economy. It is one that taxes constituents fairly and assures a revenue stream sufficient to sustain its programs and investments. If those services are not provided in an uninterrupted and dependable manner, then the economy cannot function smoothly. That represents government failure.

In the process of transitioning and emerging from an agrarian economy to one of industry, the role of capital and the use of plant and equipment, became more critical. Capital was the springboard to rapid industrial development of the United States economy. Not only did the role of capital provide the nation with a capacity to produce more goods, but it also led to the production of a greater variety of goods. The conversion from an agrarian to an industrial economy also led to a radical change in the socioeconomic structure of the country. Large amounts of capital required immense wealth. Wealth begat more wealth and a separation between the scions of industry and the working class inevitably grew. On a global basis, those countries with access to large amounts of capital prospered. Those without such access, suffered.

What did Karl Marx have to say about the economy of the 19ᵗʰ century?

In his book *Das Capital*, Karl Marx opined that a schism existed between the bourgeoisie, owners of industry and the proletariats, the workers; that owners would exploit the workers for the sake of higher profits and that inevitably the workers would rise up and overthrow the ownership class. Subsequently, in the early 20th century when the Bolshevik Revolution overthrew the tsarist rulers of Russia, Lenin, leaning on Marxist theory, built the new Russia on the backs of the working class. Thereafter, under Stalin, the theory became corrupted and Russia became a communist nation with state control of all production and resources. The Russia economic system is referred to as a command economy, because all economic decisions are centralized.

During the 20th century, nations around the world experimented with four different economic systems:

- Capitalism, the United States economic system, which is based on private ownership of property, open, competitive markets, and free private enterprise.

- Communism, a system adopted in Russia, China, and Cuba, which places ownership of all productive means and all resources in the hands of the state, in which there are no open, competitive markets or private enterprise, and in which, through a central planning organization, all production is determined by the central government and resources are allocated so as to achieve the centrally planned objectives.

- Fascism, a system adopted in Italy after World War I, whereby state and corporate powers were merged. Corporations remained private while authority over the use of productive capacity fell under the central authority of the government. This system was a butchered version of private ownership without free markets and open competition.

- Socialism, a system in which the government owns some means of production, engages in either a command or indicative form of centralized planning, and through the provision of extensive public services, paid for by high tax rates, significantly redistributes income. There is private ownership of property and open competitive markets; however the role of private enterprise is less than that in capitalist countries.

The United States has been the leading proponent of the capitalist system. The argument is that only through private ownership of resources, and open competition among independent producers and consumers can realistic costs of production be achieved, and the resulting benefits of competitive prices be made available to the consumer; That in the long-run there is a much more efficient allocation of resources to optimize the economic growth and development of a country.

Russia, which evolved into the Union of Soviet Socialist Republics (USSR) after World War II, was the leading proponent of communism, followed by China, and, as an afterthought, Cuba. While the USSR was the first to launch a spacecraft, Sputnik I, its economy never approached a goal of full employment of all resources and optimum economic growth and development. Various five-year central plans failed to allocate resources efficiently and various sectors of the economy suffered year in and year out. This problem was exacerbated by the constant tug of war between the United States and the USSR, in which both nations engaged in an arms race, one which the USSR could ill afford. In 1989, the Berlin Wall, the symbol of the USSR and Russian dominance over Eastern European satellite states, fell. Communism, in its most rigid form, collapsed with it, only to re-emerge several years later.

Fascism was briefly practiced by Italy. It was introduced during the 1930s and terminated with the end of WWII. Because of its limited history and influence on economic systems, it does not warrant further discussion.

Essentials of Macroeconomics

Socialism has thrived in many European countries. To varying degrees, it is practiced in the Scandinavian countries, Germany, France, Canada and Great Britain. The electorates of these countries have supported governments which provide extensive public programs ranging from education, social security, and unemployment benefits, to universal health. From time-to-time conservative governments have been elected in an attempt to rain in government costs and the resulting levels of taxation. However, with moderate tactical shifts and changes, the socialist economies continue unabated into the 21st century.

The decline and fall of the communist system is an unfolding tale. In many of the satellite countries, a form of socialism, with continued state planning in an indicative form, has succeeded the communist system. Russia, after a brief experimentation with private enterprise and ownership of capital, has swung back and forth between centralization and privatization. The consequences of this uncertainty have diminished the importation of direct foreign investment and the development of reliably free markets.

The great ongoing experiment is that of China. In its own uniquely determined way, the Chinese government has unleashed huge amounts of capital by creating private enterprise zones along its coastal waters. Multinational companies, together with private Chinese investors have contributed to the development of Chinese industrial capacity. At the same time, the Chinese government is continuing to exert significant control over the economy throughout the country. Where the central state does not intervene, local governments, as part of the communist party system, continue to wield significant power and control. That China is emerging as a world class power and rapidly expanding economy is undeniable.

This chapter should not be viewed as "Hail Capitalism." Rather, it should be viewed as a summary of how capitalism functions in our economy in contrast to the economic systems of other countries. Not mentioned in the discussion is the fact that during the Great Depression many intelligent people thought that capitalism had failed and that other systems, such as communism and socialism should be considered. WWII brought an end to that trend, albeit, with some political consequences in the immediate post WWII era. The student should reflect about the efficacy of the two prevailing systems, capitalism and socialism, as he/she studies the United States economic system in greater depth and bears witness to our changing global economic relationships during the 21st century.

Indeed, the current economic system in the United States might best be called social democracy. Many industries have become highly concentrated; that is four or five competitors control more than 60% of a market. Large firms, with significant economies of scale, easily render smaller firms uncompetitive. Furthermore, modern technology frequently requires huge financial capital to invest in plant, equipment, and technology.

Finally, there exist strong tendencies for firms to minimize wages, avoid paying benefits, fail to provide optimal working conditions, and ignore externalities or spillovers. To rectify these tendencies, governments have initiated and enforced regulations. Federal government departments such as Commerce, Justice, Environmental Protection, Labor, and Consumer Protection all exist to protect markets, employees, and consumers. In 1935, Social Security was introduced to the United States. In addition to providing retirement benefits, it also provided benefits to disabled workers. Medicare and Medicaid, which provide health benefits to the elderly and low-income individuals respectively, was introduced in 1965. As these programs are the initiatives of the federal government (the public sector), they are examples of socialist policies because they substitute private enterprise activities.

Within the private sector, there continue to be trends representing the consequences of unfettered capitalism; concentration, purchasing power, technological innovation, as mentioned above. There are major differences of thought and opinion among economists, elected officials and representatives of commerce and industry regarding what has become an unrelenting trend towards increased industry concentration and corresponding government intervention.

Summary

In answering the questions, what to produce, how to produce the goods and services, and how those goods and services should be distributed, the United States has evolved into a mixed economy. Rivalrous goods and services are produced by the private sector where private property, free private enterprises, the price mechanism and unfettered, competitive markets prevail. Non-rivalrous goods and services are produced by governments where accessibility and affordability are essential to an efficiently functioning economy. Trust, equity, and efficient markets are important principles to optimize both producer and consumer satisfaction. Market failure occurs when any of these principles or functions mal-functions or is abused. Various alternative forms of government, communism, fascism, and socialism have evolved and either failed or morphed into a blend of capitalism and socialism. In any event, over time, to constrain human greed and tendencies to disrupt freely competitive markets, government intervention has increased.

Moral Dilemmas

1.   Does income and wealth concentration, mentioned in the previous chapter, lead to a distortion of what is produced to satisfy tastes of high-income people and firms?

2.   Is the manner in which goods and services are produced always the most cost effective in a capitalist economy?

3.   How are the needs of the entire population assessed to assure equitable accessibility and affordability?

4.   With concentration of production in a number of industries, digital cable, cell phones, aluminum, copper, pharmaceutical, to name a few, do firms behave in a manner to create trust and equity for the consumer?

5.   In terms of accessibility and affordability, what would be some means of measuring market efficiency?

6.   Can a mixed system of both public and private sectors providing and regulating production of goods and services function effectively to optimize both producer and consumer needs?

Moral Commentary

1.   Walmart has been singled out for paying minimal wages and reducing working hours to avoid providing health benefits to its employees. With many workers forced to rely on public assistance for such services as health and childcare, the United States taxpayer effectively subsidizes Walmart. Should or should not Walmart and firms with similar policies be required to provide adequate compensation and benefits to its employees? Should the employees be left to fend for themselves?

2.   Is the price mechanism the best ultimate arbiter of who acquires a good or service? Is the price mechanism an equitable determining factor among consumers and firms of different levels of affluence? Might people of affluence cause a distortion in the price of demand both for a product and the use or resources used to manufacture the product?

3.   The United States economy has evolved from one of greater freedom of competitive markets to one with a significant role of government; albeit with most services provided by the private sector. European economies, while maintaining healthy private sectors, have vested their governments with providing more public

services, particularly in areas such as unemployment insurance, education, transportation, and health care. To a significant degree, these differences in economic systems can be attributed to cultural differences in values. Is any one system more efficient, more productive, or more innovative than another? Are the values of a population important in determining for whom an economy best performs?

Chapter 18: A Century of Economic Thinking

President Harry Truman is attributed as saying, "Give me a one-handed economist. That way he cannot say "on the other hand . . ." All of which is to say that if you put ten economists in a room you might get 20 answers to any given question. By the time you finish this chapter, your mind might be in a complete tizzy. The study of economics originally began as a study of socio-economics. As a social science, economics was incorporated with the study of sociology; how society behaves. Although starting as a study of human behavior, through twists and turns the study of economics has evolved to a quantitative analysis. This chapter will walk you through some of the theories that economists have developed to improve our ability to understand economic issues and performance.

What is the Equation of Exchange?

Gross Domestic Product (GDP) is defined as the sum total of all final goods and services produced in a year. Furthermore, GDP is measured in monetary terms. If you substitute the letter "Q" for all goods and services, and that goods and services are exchanged for money at a price "P", then the sum of the value of goods and services bought and sold is "PxQ." Now GDP = PxQ or PQ.

In addition, if money, "M" changes hands, as in the multiplier effect of money, we measure the frequency with which money changes hands and call that the velocity of money, "V." GDP = VxM or VM.

Essentials of Macroeconomics

$$GDP = PQ$$

$$GDP = VM$$

$$PQ = VM$$

The value of the Equation of Exchange is that of understanding the function of the individual parts. If prices decline and quantity stays the same, then GDP will decrease. If prices rise, but quantity stays the same, then we shall have the appearance of an increase in GDP, when it is really only a nominal or inflationary increase. In a similar vein, if the supply of money stays the same and the velocity or frequency with which money changes hands decreases, then the ability of money to facilitate transactions will result in a decrease in the level of GDP.

What is the Quantity Theory of Money?

Monetarists propound the Quantity Theory of money, which focuses on the MV components of the Equation of Exchange. In essence, the Quantity Theory examines the effect on prices of a change in the money supply or velocity. The Quantity Theory is explained with basic algebra. In any equation, if three factors are known, then the fourth factor can be solved. Therefore, for example, if "P" and "Q" and "M" are known, the "V" can be determined. $PQ = MV$, $P/V=M/Q$, $Q/M=V/P$, etc. Whatever happens to one side of the equation has an equal effect on the other side. All of this, providing that the equation has validity.

If, for example, "Q" increases and "P" does not change, then what must happen to either "M" or 'V'? Either the money supply, "M" must increase, or velocity "V" must increase. If neither occurs, then "P" will decrease. Instead of GDP increasing as a result of the increase in "Q," GDP will remain unchanged.

The question monetarists ask is, "Will the economy grow as a result of an increase in the money supply, "M," or will an increase in "M" cause an increase in inflation?" What monetarists expect is that an increase in "M" will flow through the economy by increasing spending, output, and employment. Extensive and excessive increases in "M" in the short run, however, will cause the supply curve to become vertical and consequently cause "P" to increase at inflationary levels.

What did the classical economists have to say?

Referring to chapter 2, we noted that the classical economists lived and conceived their theories in the late 18th and mid- 19th centuries. Adam Smith preached *laissez-faire* or "hands-off" the free market system. Jean-Baptiste Say preached the concept that supply creates its own demand. If people save, those savings will be invested. At low interest rates, people will save less and at high rates, they will save more. Wages and prices were thought to be downwardly flexible. During that same period, there were frequent recessions. Eventually the United States economy always recovered. The fundamental classical macroeconomic response to recessions was to do nothing. The economy would take care of itself. Classical economic theory prevailed until 1930 and the Great Depression.

Why was Keynes so revolutionary?

The Great Depression not only affected the United States. The entire world sustained a deep and prolonged recession for a period of ten years. Only afterward, as an aside, did it become known that Germany significantly mitigated its depression by embarking on a national infrastructure-building program as it prepared for war. Keynes asked the question, "Why should the federal government stand by and do nothing while the world wallows in misery?"

Keynes created the concept of aggregate demand by which he meant consumer spending, investor spending, government spending and net exports. Logically, if consumer spending and investor spending declined, then the federal government should step in to fill the gap and spend more. The government could print or borrow money and by spending it would create new employment, which, in turn, would increase demand and cause the private sector to invest and increase output. Once the economy recovered, the government tax revenue would increase and the debt incurred could be repaid.

To the monetarists Keynes argued that the nature of the depression was so deep that an increase in the money supply, "M" would not lead to inflation, but rather be spent by the poor on necessities or saved by the rich until interest rates rose to a level to attract more savings.

Indeed, in fits and starts during the depression the United States government embarked on a number of aggressive spending programs. Unfortunately, no program was sufficient in either amount or duration to pull the economy out of the depression. Keynes' theories proved to be applicable, but were not tested to their logical conclusion. It took WWII to pull the U.S. out of the depression.

Did Keynes kill monetarism?

No! The importance of monetary theory as an exclusive explanation of economic behavior or as the unique approach to resolving economic problems diminished, but it did not go away.

Exhaustive analysis of statistical data substantiates that there is a direct relationship between inflation and the money supply. Periods of inflation have been accompanied by rapid increases in the money supply. When the money supply increased more moderately, there was no inflation.

What are the basic propositions of monetarism?

1. A constant rate of increase in the money supply is essential to stable economic growth. The Fed is charged with maintaining stable economic

growth and restraining inflation. The actions of the Federal Open Market Committee (FOMC) in attempting to manage both the economy and inflation have been imprecise. In fact, swings in the economy over the years since WWII suggest that when the Fed held back increases in the money supply, the nation entered periods of recession followed by inflation, and when the Fed eased off, that is, allowed the money supply to increase gradually, inflation diminished and the economy recovered.

2. Expansionary monetary policy will only temporarily depress interest rates. If the FOMC buys Treasuries to increase the money supply, in the short-run interest rates will decline. Remember: Buying Treasuries is a transaction where the Fed pays cash and receives bonds. The increase in bond purchases causes the price of the bonds to rise. Since the coupon on the bonds is fixed in amount, the interest rate or yield on the bond decreases. However, should the effort to increase the money supply be excessive and for a longer duration, inflation will likely result, leading to increased rates of interest.

3. Expansionary monetary policy will only temporarily reduce the unemployment rate. If a modest increase in the money supply causes interest rates to decrease, then it is logical that consumers will borrow to spend more, that firms will invest and increase their output. The result will be to increase employment. If, however, the increase in the money supply is not moderate, but rather excessive with the result of inflation, then unemployment will resurface.

4. Expansionary fiscal policy, that is changes in taxation and government spending, will only temporarily raise output and employment. In order to increase spending, the government must borrow money. According to the monetarists, the increased borrowing by the government drives up interest rates, causing the private sector to withdraw. This theoretical

"crowding out" effect decreases the ability of the private sector to borrow and invest at reasonable rates of return. Mind you, the "crowding out" effect assumes that there are no additional funds available in the market. In the short-run, as public spending reverses the recessionary trend and the economy recovers, new tax revenue will enable the government to repay its obligations and by so doing cause interest rates to decline. Monetarists argue, rightly or wrongly, that consumers will not borrow at the reduced rates for purposes of buying goods and services. Consequently, aggregate demand will not increase over time.

What is the monetary rule?

The monetary rule dictates that the money supply should be increased at a constant rate. The question is, does this make sense during every phase of a business cycle and for all business cycles regardless of dimension or duration? The answer is perhaps no, but, in fact, for a number of years the Fed has focused on the size of the money supply as a means of influencing the target rate of Fed Funds (those funds loaned and borrowed among banks to manage liquidity). This practice has, by and large, been successful.

What is supply-side economics?

Fiscal policy that emphasizes a reduction in taxes and an increase in spending to reverse economic decline is referred to as demand-push economics. The reason for this description is that the increased spending by the government generates increased income to the hands of workers, who then spend their money, thus increasing the demand for goods and services.

Supply-side economics is a theory that by reducing taxes the cost of doing business will be reduced for firms that will then increase their output. To increase output, firms will employ more individuals resulting in increased spending, and as the term "trickle down" suggests, there will be general economic expansion. Empirically, the theory has never been proven to work.

Is there a point at which marginal personal income taxes are too high?

The question arises, at what point will individuals stop working because too much of their paychecks go to pay taxes? To appreciate this question, it is necessary to understand that tax rates are not applied uniformly to all levels of income. Rather, the United States income tax code is structured on the basis of marginal incremental increases. As one's income increases, the tax rate increases at various stages and the new level does not apply to lower levels or stages. Consequently, if one chooses, one could stop working because too much of one's labors would be devoted to paying taxes. Clearly, the thrust of the argument is to place a limit on the marginal tax rate so as to maximize worker output.

Coincidently, those in the higher income brackets are also those who tend to save the most. A high marginal tax rate would cause individuals to save less and thus avoid accumulated wealth and the attendant higher taxes. While in theory this also argues for lower marginal tax rates, when the rates were reduced there was no measurable change in the amounts saved or invested.

High marginal tax rates cause inefficiencies in productive market exchanges. If an individual determines not to work because of the high marginal tax rate, does that work go unperformed? Or, conversely, might another individual be hired to perform the work? That is, might the refusal to continue to work create an opportunity for another person. In point of fact, even when marginal taxes reached 90% in the 1950s and early 1960s, there was no evidence of people declining to continue to work.

Arthur Laffer, an economist, created a graph of the reverse effect of high marginal tax rates on total tax revenue. Without arguing the precision of the *Laffer Curve*, his point was that people would stop working at a certain point because of the high marginal tax rate. In effect they would be working more for the government than for themselves. The consequence of this "inaction" would be to reduce tax revenues. By reducing marginal tax rates, Laffer concluded, total government revenue would, in fact, increase. Historically, there is no evidence that people stop working because of high marginal tax rates.

Laffer Curve

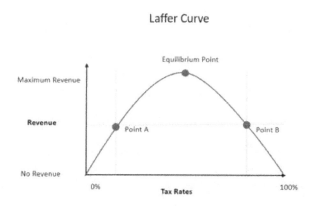

"A" represents a point on the curve where an individual will continue to work even in the face of increased marginal tax rates. Equilibrium is the point on the curve where marginal taxes are the maximum an individual will tolerate. "B" thereby represents the diminishing output resulting from high marginal taxes.

Who are the rational expectationists?

Rational expectationists are people who follow fiscal and monetary policy makers and anticipate changes in policy. By intervening and taking actions prior to the actual implementation of new policies, they, in effect, nullify the intended influence of the changes.. They believe that it is idle chatter to think that intervention to ward off inflation or jump-start the economy is a waste of time. The theory of rational expectation holds to the following beliefs:

Essentials of Macroeconomics

1. That individuals and firms anticipate consequences of changes in fiscal and monetary policy.
2. That individuals and firms act instantaneously to protect themselves.
3. That all markets are purely competitive.

Are the beliefs rational in and of themselves? Do individuals and firms act with uniformity in anticipation of policy changes, or is information asymmetrical with people having different interpretations and reactions? If actions are in anticipation, how can they be instantaneous? Are markets purely competitive when (a) they are global; (b) they have distortions attributable to size, purchasing power and access to resources; (c) they are riddled with contracts, unions, regulatory intervention; and (d) they are subject to changes in the business cycle?

What changes in economic theory have occurred in the 21st century?

Consistent with supply-side economics, in the early 21st century, taxes were significantly reduced. Once again, the theory was that with a lower marginal tax rate people would have a greater incentive to work.

Behavioral economists, those who think that human conduct has a significant influence on economic outcomes, promoted the thought that people do not act rationally and in fact make irrational and emotional decisions. Contrary to Adam Smith who argued that by acting in their own self-interest, people caused the economy to perform well. Behaviorists argue that, as human beings, people are myopic and overconfident in their predictive skills, often leading to dire consequences.

In 2019, Stephanie Kelton, Professor of Public Policy and Economics at Stony Brook University resurrected Modern Monetary Policy originally presented by Abba Lerner early in the 20th century. Why? After years of resisting the use of debt to finance federal government expenditures, in 2017, the administration granted extensive tax cuts while also increasing expenditures during a very prolonged period of economic expansion. With increasing deficits and the resulting increase in the national debt, economists expressed increasing concern.

Professor Kelton argued that because United States debt is denominated in the dollar, that is the official currency of the country, there was no reason to be concerned. Fiscal policy designed to increase employment could be financed with new money, either by borrowing or printing. In the event of an increase in inflation, taxes could be increased or bonds could be sold to decrease the money supply. Because the government is denominated in dollars there is no probability of default.

Countries which have applied this theory, Venezuela, Argentina, Brazil, Zimbabwe, to name a few, have suffered hyper-inflation, uncontrolled increases in interest rates, and total loss of value of local currency as a result.

To fight recessions, what conventional macroeconomic policies are applied?

The word conventional suggests a general agreement. Among economists, as this chapter has outlined, there is no truly unanimously agreed upon solution to economic issues. In this context, the following outlines the closest one can come to "conventional policies."

- Fiscal policy to reduce taxes and increase government spending, or increase taxes and reduce spending, depending on the business cycle.
- Monetary policy to increase the money supply and reduce interest rates, or the reverse, once again, depending on the business cycle.

The dilemmas presented by the above solutions are that they are counterproductive. To increase spending the government must borrow funds, which tends to increase interest rates. The simultaneous implementation of a fiscal policy of increased spending and a monetary policy of increasing the money supply has the potential of creating a new wave of inflation.

To fight inflation, what conventional macroeconomic policies are applied?

Does inflation necessarily accompany recessions? Since 1957 inflation has been an integral part of the problem of combating recessions. Think about it. As the economy contracts, firms allow inventories to run-off and slow down production. At the same time both fiscal and monetary policy call for injecting money into the economy. When the economy begins to recover, consumers have increased purchasing power when the supply of goods has diminished. The excess of demand over supply causes prices to rise and thus we have inflation.

One solution to this inevitability is to avoid having the federal government and the Fed simultaneously increase earnings and the money supply. One or the other should hold back. In fact, this practice has been applied with considerable success, but not without some pain on the part of the unemployed.

The globalization of financial markets has impeded conventional macroeconomic policy considerably. Both the government, through fiscal policy management, and the Fed through monetary policy management can influence domestic markets. When foreign investors, both public and private, determine to invest or disinvest in United States Treasuries or other debt instruments, those activities may interfere with domestic policies and produce undesirable results.

Summary

As mentioned at the beginning of this chapter there is a dizzying array of philosophies and theories among economists. Some economists are rigidly quantitative in their approach. Some are on the opposite extreme of arguing that behavior, rational or not, drives the economy. Some argue for active intervention on the part of the government and the Fed, and some argue for total abstinence by both bodies. In the end, when swings in the economy occur, both the government and the Fed tend to intervene in order to reduce the potential of prolonged, deep recessions and to promote economic growth, reduced unemployment, and maintain price stability.

Moral Dilemmas

1.   Adam Smith's humanistic view of people acting out of self-interest contributed to economic well-being. That theory was developed in the late 18th century. Does it continue to apply in the 21st century?

2.   Policies designed to modify economic conditions, recession, inflation, and expansion affect the general population differently; some benefit, some suffer. Should specific measures be undertaken to limit those who benefit, or provide relief for those who suffer? What measures might you suggest?

3.   Are there times when the government should do nothing; that is, let economic conditions sort themselves out? Is this responsible behavior?

Moral Commentary

1.   With the growth of international trade, with the integration of global supply lines, with the increase in financial inter-dependency, and with increased technological interdependence, national economic policies must take into consideration both domestic and foreign impacts; and both direct and indirect consequences. This raises the question of priorities: Who should come first, those at home or those abroad, or can all parties be given equal consideration?

2.   Economic analysts and economic policy makers tend to think in short-term time frames with respect to economic policy making. How can the business cycle be expanded? How can recessions be avoided or minimized? While long-

term trends are measured and evaluated, the intention is to make the road to long-term growth smooth and unimpeded, while preserving businesses and industries which have minimum long-term prospects. Coal consumption versus solar and wind generation serve as an example. Landline telephones versus cell phones serve as another. The important issues to be addressed are what changes are in process and virtually inevitable, and who will be impacted by those changes, both positively and negatively?

Chapter 19: Debt and Equity and Shadow Banking

What is a debt?

Debts are financial obligations which are owed by borrowers to investors or lenders. Total global public and private debt is approximately one hundred eight-eight trillion dollars. That's $188,000,000,000,000. Total global gross domestic product is estimated at eighty trillion dollars. That's $80,000,000,000,000. Of the former, public debt is about $60 trillion and private debt about $129 trillion. Compare that with the total global gross domestic product (GDP) of $67 trillion. Of the latter, the US GDP is about $21 trillion, China $12 trillion, and Japan $5 trillion. By the time you read this, all of the above numbers will have changed both in absolute amounts and relative to one another.

What are equities?

Equities are financial instruments which represent ownership in a firm or enterprise. Equities are not measured on the basis of the book value of a firm or enterprise. Rather, equities are measured in terms of market capitalization; that is the price or value at which a stock is traded in the marketplace. Total global market capitalization is estimated at $67 trillion, of which the United States' share is $30 trillion.

If you find these numbers mind-boggling, join the crowd. They come from a variety of sources: The United Nations, The World Bank, The Bank for International Settlements, The Economist, and the US Department of Labor.

What are insurance policies?

Insurance policies are third party commitments to reimburse the policyholder, or his or her designated beneficiary for losses sustained and contractually covered by the policy. Insurance companies are regulated by states and are required to meet certain financial conditions to qualify to do business in a particular state. Insurance companies issue policies to cover the following risks: Loss of life, Disability caused by loss of a functioning body part or mind, Loss or damage to property caused by fire, flood, earthquake, accidents, Liability for injuries suffered by individuals on one's property, Auto damage to another party's auto or one's own, and health care. These are numerous but do not represent all types of insurance. The point is that insurance policies are designed to mitigate against loss or provide relief. They are not designed to enrichen.

What has changed in the world of debts and equities?

Chapters eleven and twelve, Money and Banking, and The Federal Reserve and Monetary Policy address the world of finance as it existed until the 1990s. Traditionally, banks served as financial intermediaries. That is, banks served as a lubricant to the economy. Money was not an end in and of itself, but rather a means to an end. Currency, which in our case is a commodity called the United States dollar, is issued by the Federal Reserve as an obligation of the United States of America which states "This note is legal tender for all debts public and private." The money supply, M2 consists of currency, demand deposits, savings accounts, money market mutual funds, and time deposits up to $100,000. The Federal Reserve Bank, which regulates the banking system's ability to create money, focuses on this number.

During the depression, the Congress determined that commercial banking, to include consumer banking, should be legally separated from the powers to perform investment banking services. The Glass-Steagall Banking Act of 1933 formally prohibited commercial banks from engaging in investment banking activities. Those activities included underwriting public offerings of private entities, corporations, or investing in private enterprise securities, to include stocks and bonds. The purpose was to strengthen bank financial statements by prohibiting banks from being both lenders to and shareholders of the same clients.

In 1995, Congress passed and the President signed the Gramm-Leach-Bliley Act, which repealed the prohibitions of Glass-Steagall. The effect of this legislation was to create a new industry which became an end in and of itself: Finance. Banks, which had concentrated in money creation, lending or credit extensions, could now participate in the issuance of equities, the purchase and sale of equities and other real financial assets, and the issuance and trading of new instruments called derivatives.

What are derivatives?

Real assets are defined as those assets which are tangible. Examples are: Real estate, machinery and equipment, chattels, and contractual financial obligations, such as consumer loans, mortgage loans, credit card debts, and short-term and long-term loans to individuals and firms. These are the types of assets addressed in chapter four, Investments. Derivatives are financial instruments whose value is a reflection or dependent on the value of a related real asset. For example, a farmer plants a field of corn. The corn takes five months to mature and ripen. At the time he or she plants the corn, the farmer has no idea what the price of corn will be in five months. To avoid speculation or the risk of a very low price, the farmer contracts to deliver the corn in five months at a price determined upon executing the contract. No matter what the actual price may be in five months, when the farmer delivers the corn, he/she is paid at the price set in the futures contract. Because that contract is dependent on the market price of corn, it is a derivative contract.

It is important to note that in the above example there are two parties, the party who initiates the contract and the counterparty, who responds. Each has a different view of the market. The farmer fears corn prices may decline. The counterparty expects prices to increase. They settle on a price satisfactory to both parties.

Another example is that of a United States citizen who purchases a Mercedes Benz 450SL in January, for delivery in Stuttgart in June. The price of the MB 450SL is euros 100,000. Upon taking delivery, the US individual will have to pay the seller those euros. The question arises, how many dollars will it take to buy euros 100,000 at the time of delivery? To minimize the risk that the value of the euro to the dollar may increase over time, the buyer contracts to purchase the euros at the time he/she commits to buy the car for delivery in June at a price set in January. That is a futures contract and a derivative contract because it is based on the real market cost of the euro currency in January.

How large is the derivative market?

While banks and other financial entities have fought furiously to avoid having derivative contracts treated as insurance products, in reality, that is what they are. The function of a derivative contract is to enable an individual or firm with a real asset at risk; that is an asset whose value may decrease over time such as the farmer's corn or the auto buyer's dollars. The dispute regarding classification is specifically to avoid regulation. Derivatives are traded both on exchanges, such as the Chicago Board of Trade, or over-the-counter. Regardless, trading is opaque. The size and terms of contracts, including buyers and sellers is not disclosed. While confidentiality of any transaction is always an issue of privacy, the lack of transparency makes it very difficult to measure the volume of contracts, the range of prices of contracts, and who the parties and counterparties are, those being the participants in the market.

Derivative contracts are recorded with reference to their <u>notional value</u>. The best way to define notional value is to provide an example. The largest volume, estimated at $200 trillion, is composed of interest rate swaps. Two unrelated parties have each borrowed $1 million, payable in ten years. Party (A) has borrowed at a variable rate of Prime plus three percent (assuming 2020 rates of 3.25% + 3% = 6.25%). The rate on the loan will change from time-to-time as the prime rate changes. Party (B) has borrowed at a fixed rate of 6%. The rate will not change for the life of the loan. Party (A) is concerned that over the next ten years, interest rates will increase. He/she might wind up paying 7, 8, or 9%. In the meantime, party (B) is concerned that rates will decrease. He/she will wind up paying 6% in a market where interest rates might be 5 or 4%. To satisfy the two disparate outlooks or expectations, the parties enter into an interest rate swap. They each continue to owe the $1 million, but party (A) assumes the obligation to pay interest at the fixed rate, and party (B) assumes the obligation to pay interest at the variable rate. How do you value the amount of financial obligation borne by each party? The risk or exposure is the payment of interest, but without reference to the underlying contracts, that is the $1 million, there is no way to determine the amount of each parties' exposure. Therefore, the contracts are recorded using their notional value; that of the principal value of the underlying contract.

All in, the derivative market is estimated at ten times global gross domestic product, or $670 trillion. By volume the two largest contracts traded are foreign exchange currency futures and interest rate swaps.

What other types of derivatives are traded?

There is an alphabet soup of derivative products. Below is a sample list:

- Interest Rate Swaps: described above
- Currency swaps or currency futures: described above
- CDOs: Collateralized Debt Obligations, Bonds which are secured by corporate debt, and consumer debt such as credit card debt, or auto financial paper
- CDSs: Credit Default Swaps: An instrument that pays the holder an amount relating to the non-payment of a debt of a specified obligation
- MBS: Mortgage Backed Security: Bonds which are secured by an underlying bundle of individual mortgages with maturities ranging from 10 to 30 years.
- Stock or equity options: Contracts giving the buyer the right, but not the obligation to buy (call) or sell (put) a stock at a predetermined (strike) price over a specified period of time.

In a positive sense, the creation of all of the above instruments or vehicles added significant capacity to credit markets. They also added a means of diversifying risk. Through trading these negotiable instruments, investors could enter and exit the market, purchase or sell the derivatives at will.

Mortgage Backed Securities were first created back in 1985; however, they did not become aggressively structured and issued until the 1990s. Prior to that time, home buyers were dependent on traditional lending institutions: Savings Banks, Credit Unions, Commercial Banks, the Federal Home Loan Mortgage Corporation and Federal National Mortgage Association. That was sufficient to finance a housing stock of 83 thousand in 1980, and 116 thousand in 2000, but not 140 thousand in 2020. That is an increase of 69%, or an annual rate of increase of 1.8% p.a. over the 30-year period. Mortgage backed securities attracted a host of new investors to the financial markets and enabled the financing of 24 thousand additional homes but provided competitive financing for refinancing of existing stock at ever increasing price levels. This, among other instruments, is what gave rise to shadow banking.

What is shadow banking?

While at first glance the word "shadow" may appear pejorative, that is not the intent. Shadow banking is defined as those institutions, firms or individuals who engage in investing, lending, or borrowing outside of the normal, regulated framework. The instruments include securitization, (CDOs, MBSs, CDSs) derivatives, and money market funds, for example. The participants include investment banks, hedge funds, mutual funds, firms and individuals.

How did banking and the world of finance become an end rather than a means to an end?

Back to the beginning of this chapter. Look at the numbers: Public and private debt: $188 trillion. Global GDP: $67 trillion. Global derivatives: $670 trillion. Of the latter, more than 220 thousand contracts are traded daily. Derivative traders generate income through the difference between what the buyer pays (bid) and the price the seller accepts (ask). In a matter of seconds, for a contract valued at $ 1 million, at a price differential of .2 %, that is 20 basis points or 2/10th of 1 %, a trader generates $2,000 in income. Is it any wonder so many young college graduates gravitate to Wall Street to work?

The development of this enormous financial market has contributed to the rapid growth and expansion of major and minor firms in the US. and globally. Access to affordable financial capital, the ability to diversify and mitigate risk is indeed a vital part of the evolving U.S and global economies.

How have the policies and activities of the Federal Reserve evolved over time?

From its establishment in 1913, and throughout the 20th century, the Federal Reserve (the Fed) has been a bankers' bank. As described in chapter twelve, its role has been that of regulator, custodian of a safe and sound banking system, guardian of a growing, stable economy, and, through open market operations, manager of interest rates and bank liquidity.

With the advent of the 21st century, and faced with the continued growth of shadow banking, the increase in the size of financial markets, and the dependence of multiple industries, firms, and individuals on economic and financial stability, the Fed has become a banker of last resort. Its policies and activities have expanded beyond the traditional banking system to that of assuring liquidity and stability in the entire and complex financial markets. To fulfill its expanded role, the Fed has intervened in financial markets to purchase and sell not only United States Treasury obligations but also a variety of instruments issued by the private sector. The Fed, at this writing, had a balance sheet of $17 trillion or the equivalent of 80% of GDP.

How has the Fed expansion of market intervention tools evolved?

The dramatic change in Fed policies and actions actually began in 2008, when in response to a housing or mortgage induced recession, the Fed introduced quantitative easing (QE). In three rounds, QE1, QE2, and QE3, the Fed acquired $1.7 trillion of bank debts, mortgage backed securities, and treasury obligations. Unquestionably, the process restored confidence to banks and financial markets, and helped ease the economy out of a great recession. Subsequently, with the sudden and unanticipated threat of Covid19, the coronavirus, and its impact on social and economic activity, the increase of unemployment to 17% and a decrease in GDP of 7%, the Fed reintroduced quantum easing. This time around, as described above, the Fed expanded the number and types of financial instruments it was willing to acquire. At this writing, the outcome is too early to predict.

Summary

The traditional forms of financing private sector enterprises through equity and debt has exploded into increased reliance on debt to finance corporate expansion, acquisition and equity reduction. Total global private sector debt is $129 trillion. To mitigate risk for holders of debt instruments, a host of new products called derivatives has emerged:

- Interest rate swaps to protect against unanticipated shifts in prevailing rates
- Currency swaps to diminish foreign exchange rate risks
- Collateralized Debt Obligations to increase holdings and diversify risk
- Credit Default Swaps to insure against non-payment of debt instruments

Banking regulations changed to eliminate prohibitions and permit banks to engage in investment banking activities and to participate in broader financial markets. Non-regulated financial entities, referred to as shadow banking, emerged to have a significant influence on markets and economic performance. To fulfill its role as the central bank of the United States, the Fed expanded its policies and actions to include broader market intervention through acquisition of more debt instruments.

Moral Dilemmas

1.   Should corporate managers succumb to low market interest rates by burdening their firms with substantial debt to be repaid far in the future?

2.   What responsibilities do managers have to protect stakeholders against unanticipated threats by maintaining strong levels of equity?

3.   By aggressively intervening in financial markets, is the fed propping up otherwise failing enterprises, both financial and non-financial in structure?

Moral Commentary

1.   There were multiple causes of the financial market failure in 2008. Among them were massive levels of mortgage defaults by homeowners, whose debts exceeded the value of their homes. The quick and easy solution to preserving market liquidity and protecting against bank failures was for the Fed to acquire the mortgage backed securities. Should the government have provided more direct relief to the homeowners?

2.   Do the Fed actions of increasing its balance sheet to $17 trillion by acquiring a broader range of financial instruments directly or indirectly provide inducements for both issuers and investors to continue their reliance on this form of corporate expansion?

Chapter 20: Threats, Opportunities, and Uncertainty

In the past fifty years, the United States and many countries around the world have experienced one form of financial and economic crisis or another. Six major crises were:

- 1976 – 1981, The US experienced rapidly increasing inflation to peak in 1980 at 13.5% with unemployment reaching 10.7%
- 1980s, Latin American countries experienced a foreign debt crisis
- 1997, Asian countries, beginning in Southeast Asia, experienced a major currency crisis
- 1990s, New England states experienced near depression levels of economic contraction
- 2007, Sparked by mortgage-backed securities failure, the US entered a major recession
- 2020, Ignited by coronavirus, the world entered a recession in February

Positive and negative events, opportunities and threats, may be classified as either endogenous or exogenous; that is generated from within or originating from the outside. Let's elaborate on the above examples:

What caused the inflation and unemployment of 1976 -1981?

The 1976 – 1981 crisis may be characterized as exogenous in its origins. After a post WWII period of economic expansion, in 1973 a global cartel of petroleum exporting countries in a unified and coordinated effort, initiated an oil embargo causing prices to increase from $3 per barrel to nearly $12 or 400%. In 1979, what are known as the Yom Kippur War between Israel and neighboring states, and the Iranian Revolution, caused further disruptions in oil supplies. By 1980, oil prices had reached $35 per barrel. These price shocks contributed to a downturn in production in housing, steel and automobiles. The resulting stagflation, a combination of increased inflation and unemployment, lead to a recession. Actions of the Federal Reserve to slow the growth of the money supply and allow interest rates to increase eventually brought the economy back to stability.

What factors contributed to the Latin American debt Crisis?

The Latin American debt crisis was a combination of both endogenous and exogenous factors. With a significant dependency on a healthy United States economy, the United States recessions of the late 1970s and early 1980s eventually came home to roost in Latin America. In addition, the United States and other international banks, faced with a glut of funds emanating from the OPEC countries and their new-found wealth, loaned generous sums to governments of developing countries. When the cost of debt service exceeded their respective economic output levels, countries such as Argentina, Brazil, and Mexico defaulted on their debts. The crisis was resolved through a combination of efforts to restructure the debts by the International Monetary Fund (IMF), various foreign governments and private international banks.

What events contributed to the Asian currency crisis?

The Asian Currency Crisis of 1979 began with the inability of the Thai government to support its currency, the baht, and thus allowing it to float, that is freely traded. This might be characterized as an endogenous factor, but the ramifications on countries throughout Southeast Asia and Asia were certainly exogenous. As it turned out, the currency collapse led to a falling like a house of cards. The inter-relationship of the baht to other currencies revealed that parties and counterparties to foreign exchange or currency transactions were inextricably intertwined. The failure of one currency led to a crisis in Indonesia, South Korea and then in Hong Kong, Laos, Malaysia, and the Philippines. Once again, the IMF led a recovery process with loans of $40 billion to South Korea, Thailand, and Indonesia. By 1999 the economies of Southeast Asia and Asia began to show signs of recovery.

Why was New England's recession different from that of the nation?

Was the severe recession experienced by the New England states in the early 1990s endogenous or exogenous? As a region, New England suffered more than the rest of the nation. During the 1980s, New England, especially Connecticut and Massachusetts, enjoyed economic expansion. Among other things, real estate prices increased rapidly. Much of Connecticut's growth was attributable to increased demand for military goods. In the case of Massachusetts, the growth was in financial services and hi-technology. From 1990 – 1991, the U.S. entered a mild recession, mostly attributed to a monetary restricting policy of the Fed. Unemployment rose and GDP decreased. With the reduction in military related production, Connecticut lost 190,000 jobs. Similar contractions in Massachusetts also led to a much more severe recession. General recovery of the nation as a whole eventually dragged New England along with it. Clearly, the answer to the question was that both endogenous and exogenous factors contributed to the crisis and its solution.

What were the causes and consequences of the 2007 great recession?

Referring back to chapter 19, Debt, Equity, and Shadow Banking, financial market failure led to the great recession of 2007. More specifically, the total sum of derivative instruments issued, traded and held by major financial institutions to include, banks, investment banks, mutual funds, and hedge funds suffered a loss of market confidence. The initial blow was the failure or default of mortgages collateralizing mortgage backed securities. As though a mountain of dominos, once one MBS failed, it was only a matter of time before many others failed as well. Then, like a pandemic, the failure virus infected other instruments: CDOs, and CDSs. The economic consequences of excessive household debt and unemployment of 8.7 million followed. To stem the hemorrhaging, the Fed intervened by offering up to $500 billion to guarantee investments to the FDIC. Federal government spending programs increased from 19% of GDP to 24%. The recession ended in 2009; however, GDP did not return to pre-2007 levels until May 2014. This is a classic endogenous event. The great recession also triggered a failure of two of the three largest domestic producers of cars and truck: General Motors and Chrysler/Fiat. The federal government injected $700 billion to the car makers taking debt and equity instruments as collateral. Eventually, they totally repaid the government.

Why would a new virus, Covid19, cause economic disruption?

Disease and pestilence have been major threats to society or civilization since the origins of humankind. In the beginning of the 20th century, the disease was the Spanish Flu. In the 1930s and 1940s, the disease was polio. Today, infants are vaccinated at an early age to immunize them from whooping cough, measles, chicken pox, and polio. In the past 20 years a variety of flus have originated in Asian countries, resulting in the annual development of vaccines designed to treat each specific variety of flu. Towards the end of 2019, a new and more virulent strain emerged in China. Because of large movements of people within China, and the great number of people who travel by air to and from China, it was not long before the virus reached Europe and eventually, the United States. Many of those who contracted the disease suffered very debilitating effects, and approximately 4% of those infected died. Without adequate testing, and with the lack of a preventive vaccine, vast numbers of people were told not to work and to stay at home until the spread of the virus abated. The economic impact was to cause unemployment that affected 30 million people or 19% of the labor force. The Fed stepped in to assure stability in financial markets, and the federal government, together with state governments provided unemployment insurance and outright payments to people with incomes of less than $120,000. This is a classic exogenous event, and the outcome is yet to be determined.

So much about threats or negative events. What about positive or opportunistic events?

Over the same period of time, fifty years, a number of discoveries, innovations, and events occurred to spur economic growth. Six examples are:

- 1989, Collapse of the Berlin Wall
- 1991, the creation of the euro
- 1990s invention and release of the World Wide Web
- 1990s, rapid expansion of private, commercial satellites
- 2000s, miniaturization and mass production of cell phones
- 2000s, massive innovation and application of robot technology

Three of the above examples had exogenous effects on nations and economies far outside the former Soviet Union, the seventeen nations comprising the euro zone, and the global spread of the World Wide Web. The remaining three are clearly endogenous events.

What were the causes and effects of the collapse of the Berlin Wall?

The collapse of the Berlin Wall was more symbolic than substantive. The Soviet Union was the result of the division of responsibility and governance of nations overwhelmed and occupied by Nazi Germany during WWII. Immediately after the war, Russia occupied and controlled fifteen eastern, central European and Balkan states. However, by 1989, the seat of Soviet power, the Kremlin, was no longer able to govern the largest union in geographic size and cultural and linguistic diversity, or to provide for the basic economic necessities while simultaneously building a huge war machine. As a result, there were numerous attempted insurrections and eventual political and economic failure. Soviet Union dissolved and fifteen independent republics arose. The return to freedom and release of new-found energy lead to economic recovery and expansion of many, but not all of the fifteen newly formed nations.

What gave rise to the formation of a common currency called the euro?

Immediately after WWII six European countries formed the European Coal and Steel Community. This was a joint effort to regulate industrial production as a step towards European unification. The notion that countries that develop strong trade relations and greater interdependency are unlikely to go to war was a driving force. Eventually, twenty-seven countries joined to form a common market or trade union called the European Common Market. Twenty-seven countries meant 27 different currencies, and prior to the formation of the union, 27 trade barriers, 27 customs, and 27 different governments intervening in commerce. The union lacked a single currency to ease the movements of goods, services and people. Nineteen countries comprise the euro zone, which today has a population of 342 million and a GDP of $13 trillion. With one central bank, monetary policies and regulations are initiated affecting all nineteen members. For lack of having a common fiscal policy, there continue to be challenges; however, the positive benefits have met and exceeded expectations.

What would the world look like without the World Wide Web?

The World Wide Web (WWW) was invented and introduced in 1991. It was preceded by the invention of the internet in 1965. Through use of common technology, public, private, corporate and individual users can communicate via computers across the globe. The number of innovations and enhancements, such as Wi-Fi, clouds for data processing and storage, streaming, browsers, and the list goes on and on. The WWW may not have shrunk the world, but it certainly has increased communication, productivity, inter-dependency, and nurtured research, invention, innovation, and creativity.

What is the difference between public and private satellites?

Satellite technology development was and is very expensive. Governments led the pack with defense and other public functions serving as the major incentives to develop such technology. Satellites provide global surveillance, communication, guidance systems, and weather forecasts. Currently, there are more than 2,000 satellites orbiting the globe. The private sector has more satellites in orbit than the public. Some are geo-stationary, while others maintain continuous orbits. Satellites serve cell phone networks, provide data to farmers, track storms, fires, shifts in ecological activity, and traffic movement by air, land, and sea; once again, the list goes on and on.

Who owns a cell phone?

The answer to that question is probably better answered by asking, who does not own a cell phone. From the wealthiest entrepreneur to the humble Indian tuk tuk driver, cell phones are ubiquitous. The earliest cell phones were large, bulky and required a transmitter in addition to the hand-held device. When Nokia, a Finnish company, developed the miniature technology at affordable costs, the popularity of cell phones spread like wildfire. When Google developed android technology and Apple the iPhone, smartphones replaced the now obsolete cell phone. This is another example of creative destruction. The modern smartphone has more capability than the first IBM computer, which was temperature sensitive with 12,500 vacuum tubes, and occupied an entire climate-controlled room. Microchip technology changed the world of computers and was an essential innovation to lead to today's smartphone. The total effects on commercial and interpersonal communications have yet to be fully realized and measured.

What is robot technology?

The industrial revolution commenced when humankind figured out how to substitute machinery or devices to replace man and animal power. When people learned how to harness boiling water by capturing the steam and converting the energy to drive a cylinder and therefore pump water, there was no end in sight of the possibilities. In a sense, robot technology, which is the application of design and production of a machine or instrument that will reproduce the same movements rapidly, efficiently and accurately, is no more than the logical extension of the industrial revolution begun 250 years ago. Artificial technology has enabled the development of robots to perform actions not previously imagined. Applications include industrial production, farming, mining, laboratory research, medical procedures; and the list goes on.

What is uncertainty?

Uncertainty is the lack of predictability of forthcoming events, behavior or responses and outcomes due to imperfect or unknown information. All of the above twelve cited events were unexpected, unpredictable and led nations and economies to react or adjust in different manners and with different results. Uncertainty is always with us. Uncertainty breeds a lack of trust.

How do a nation and an economy deal with uncertainty?

There is no single answer to this question. There are multiple factors ranging from the form, strength, and reliability of government, the range of public services available to the public, the presence of a reliable system of justice, accessibility and affordability of public health, universal education, a stable, well-functioning economy, and finally transparent access to accurate and timely data and information.

Three indices or measures of relative degree of freedom, effective and equitable systems of justice, and ease of doing business might provide some insight into a nation's development, resilience, and capacity to absorb shock or deal with uncertainty. Freedom House annually publishes an index comparing degrees of exercise of freedom, where 100 is the best and close to zero the worst. The World Justice Project publishes similar data with respect to justice, with both a score, 100 being the highest, and a ranking from 1 to 128. The World Bank publishes a report on relative ease of doing business ranging from very easy (VE), to easy (E) to medium (M). In the chart below, ten countries (listed alphabetically) are compared on each of the measures. To the above is added per capita income as reported by the International Monetary Fund in US dollars (in parentheses).

Country/ Per Capita	Freedom	Justice Score	Justice Rank	Ease of Business	Rank of Ease
Canada ($46,212)	98	75	7	VE	23
China ($10,098)	10	43	88	VE	31
Finland ($49,868)	100	87	3	VE	20
Germany	94	84	6	VE	22
Iran ($5,506)	17	35	99	M	127
Japan ($40,846)	96	78	15	VE	29
North Korea	3	na	na	na	na
Saudi Arabia	7	na	na	E	62
United Kingdom	94	74	8	VE	8
United States	86	73	11	VE	6

What nation appears to have the greatest capacity to address uncertainties? You, as the beholder should be the judge. Does Finland, with consistently high scores across the board, leap out? Or because of its high per capita income, do you select the United States? Do these measures provide sufficient information, or do you need more? There is no question that more advanced countries provide an abundance of statistical data with respect to economic performance, education, health care, and crime and justice. There is also evidence that over time, for developed nations, business cycles, or economic swings have decreased in frequency and diminished in severity. Still, as evidenced with the Covid19 pandemic of 2020, there is much to be learned.

How do less developed or emerging nations address uncertainty?

Because of a lack of data, little can be said about North Korea. With a low per capita income and an unmeasured justice system, Saudi Arabia appears to be vulnerable. Add to that the fact that Saudi Arabia is dependent on a single export commodity, oil, and its vulnerability is increased. And yes, more information is required.

This chapter brings us to the conclusion of this book, and in a sense is the very reason to study macroeconomics. With all of the principles, concepts and hypothetical explorations, economics, as a behavioral science, lacks both specificity and precise predictability, such as in the cases of physics and chemistry. Does that make it useless? By no means. Macroeconomics provides a structure and discipline not only to analyze an economy and economic behavior, but also to frame questions, collect data, and formulate policies. Macroeconomics affords individuals, firms, and public sector entities the ability to make informed decisions about their respective personal, professional, and financial activities. While macroeconomics does not eliminate risk and uncertainty, it provides a framework with which to manage those factors.

Summary

Life is full of threats, opportunities, and uncertainties. This chapter outlines six examples of threats, and how they have impacted economies either as internally generated, endogenous, or externally generated, exogenous. In like manner, six examples of opportunities were also outlined. Finally, how various nations are equipped to address uncertainties is discussed, not conclusively, but rather in the form of data to be analyzed and questions to be asked. The fundamental value of studying macroeconomics rests in its structure and discipline as a social science.

Moral Dilemmas

1.   When facing inflation and looking for solutions, what questions should be raised to examine the impact of inflation on all sectors, regions, and people in the economy?

2.   If debt crises are generated by desperate pursuit of short-term solutions to economic threats, or by irresponsible financial decision-making, how can its victims prevent or mitigate possible repetitions?

3.   Should measures be taken to assure that all sectors, regions, and peoples have equal access to affordable new technology?

Moral Commentary

1.   In the United States, unrestrained economic behavior, which leads to a crisis, such as the mortgage-backed securities failure, sometimes referred to as the housing bubble, is dealt with after-the-fact. Frequently, the response is the introduction and implementation of new regulations. Is that a rational approach to solving a behavioral problem?

2.   As an amoral social science, should economists and private and public sector decision-makers even contemplate the moral consequences of their actions?

INDEX

ABOUT THE AUTHOR

Stephen Hotchkiss is Associate Professor (retired) of Notre Dame College of Ohio, where he taught economics, finance, applied ethics and emotionally intelligent leadership over a period of ten years. Prior to that he dedicated forty years to international, corporate and community banking. His twenty-five years of international banking included residencies in Venezuela, Panama, and Ecuador. He was the founding president of Citizens Community Bank of Idaho and founding co-chair of the Idaho International Choral Festival. For thirty years, he has been a trustee of a charitable trust granting millions of dollars to fund care and research in cancer and epilepsy.

Stephen Hotchkiss is a graduate of Bates College, BA, Thunderbird Graduate School of International Management, BFT, and Cleveland State University, MBA. He also studied advanced economics at the Graduate Faculty of the New School for Social Research.

Made in USA - Kendallville, IN
1184443_9798693821743
10.23.2020 0824